HOW TO SELL YOUR IDEA

How to Sell Your Idea

A COMPLETE, STEP-BY-STEP GUIDE, FROM CONCEPT TO CONTRACT

Stuart J. Kamille

This publication is designed to provide information with regard to the subject matter covered. It is sold with the understanding that this book is not intended to render specialized, legal, accounting, or other advice for which the services of a competent professional should be sought.

Copyright © 2006 Stuart J. Kamille

Printed in the United States of America

ISBN-13: 978-0-9774-7350-2
ISBN-10: 0-9774-7350-3

Published by Golden Leaf Press
Editors: Mike Sion; Todd Manza, Manza Editorial
Cover photo: Chuck Cannady Photography
Book design: Valerie Brewster, Scribe Typography
Printed by Bookmasters

CONTENTS

PART IV

Profiting from Your Idea

ACKNOWLEDGMENTS

It took me thirty years to write this book – not because it was a difficult book to write, but rather, because it took me that long to gather enough experience to make it worthwhile for you, the reader. That thirty-year lesson was filled with people and events that actually provided all the material. They wrote it; I just kept my eyes and ears open and copied it down.

To all my clients, business partners, and employees, I owe a debt of gratitude for making my career an interesting one. Without them, this book would be on an entirely different subject, if it existed at all.

The actual writing required the help of thorough professionals like my editors, Todd Manza and Mike Sion, and my book designer, Valerie Brewster and the folks at Scribe, and Bookmasters. It's difficult to take someone's scattered thoughts and somehow transform them into intelligible English that not only is organized but also is a pleasure to read. Somehow, they managed it.

My friends Ellis and Brenda Cannon, Ernie Goggio, George Gillemot, Mel Phelps, Gideon Markham, members of the faculty at the University of Georgia, and my patent attorney, Mike Mallie at Blakely Sokoloff, added many helpful facts and well-placed questions, the answers to which greatly increased the scope and value of the final product. They invested a lot of their personal time in helping me get it right. Every field has its difficulties and rewards, and their advice was invaluable.

Without Kathy, my wife, I would never have gotten to first base. Actually, I wouldn't even have gotten up to bat.

She believed that I could and should write this book, and as you will see, believing in something is what makes all the difference.

And lastly, to all of you with an idea you would like to see sold, I salute you for your spunk and creativity. I know it hasn't been easy coming up with something others should value. I believe you created your idea for a reason. Now you must give it a chance to see the light of day. Perhaps this book will help.

SJK
April 2006

FOREWORD

By Millard Phelps

Venture capitalist, semiconductor industry analyst,
and director of four privately held companies

Entrepreneurs come in two flavors: those who intend to build a complete company around a concept or invention, and those who wish to sell or license the concept or invention to someone else. Each type of entrepreneur – the company builder and the inventor with an idea to sell – is a big dreamer facing daunting challenges.

Consider the company builder. He or she has to produce a viable business plan (which will likely as not end up scrubbed or revised beyond recognition) and wrangle with venture capitalists who, if they enjoy the upper hand, could very well end up replacing the entrepreneur/founder with their own handpicked management team. And that's even before the company gets off the ground! Once seed money is committed, the feasibility, reproducibility, and reliability of the product or service loom as hurdles to surmount before follow-on financing is secured.

Given such obstacles, is it any wonder that few business ventures founded on new ideas succeed? The inventor, in contrast, would seem to have it much easier. That's because the inventor is typically spared the ordeal of creating a company to produce a product or provide a service. Therefore – one would think – the inventor has a much easier time of it. He or she must merely sell a patent-protected invention to the established engineering, manufacturing, or distribution entity in the pertinent field... and then collect license fees and an endless stream of royalties. Right? Like the creator of the Post-it or Velcro?

Not so fast!

The inventor faces unique challenges and frustrations that are anything but trivial... as this thoroughly entertaining book reveals. Readers of *How to Sell Your Idea* will at a minimum know what they are up against as inventors bringing an invention to market, and how best to prepare.

Selling an idea to a company involves a complete set of obstacles different from those faced by the entrepreneur. There are significant legal, technical, and financial challenges. But beyond those are impediments that are strictly human.

Jealousy. (Corporate executives and employees don't always appreciate creative minds.) Fear. (If a company's executives license an invention from an outsider, how can they justify their own engineering staff?) Doubt. (If a product succeeds, will it cannibalize the company's current revenue stream?)

Consider Kodak embracing digital photography while remaining hostage to film revenue. Or the Swiss watch industry seeing mechanical watches replaced by digital Japanese competitors. Is it any wonder that relatively few new inventions succeed?

Clearly, the author of this book has "been there." He's lived the life of the entrepreneur/inventor... and survived intact to tell all. Nice of him to take the time to pass along his experiences in this leave-nothing-unsaid manual for masochists.

Hats off to Stu Kamille – and all of the entrepreneurs and inventors responsible for the Yankee ingenuity that has made this nation the world power that it is!

INTRODUCTION

There are plenty of how-to books on inventing. Far too many, some would say. So why another?

Actually, this book is not about inventing at all. This book assumes you have a great idea. It begins after the lightning has struck. It's written for all you inventors who have this great idea but don't know what to do next. You know you need to do something, but what? When I started, I needed a book that would tell me that. I needed someone or something that would help explain what I should do, step by step, to bring this great idea to market.

Selling your great idea is every inventor's dream. And this book can help you do just that. *How to Sell Your Idea* tells you exactly what you must do, step by step, to develop, protect, and sell your idea. It's written by someone who has spent more than thirty years developing new products and getting them onto store shelves. I hold eight patents and I have made money from all of them. Over the years, I've learned quite a bit.

As soon as people found out that I had several patents and had successfully sold them, they started asking me for advice. After enough people asked, I decided that there was a need for what I had learned. So, what you are holding is a lot of that experience put between the covers of this book. I've tried to make it clear, understandable, and – most importantly – useful.

There is no substitute for experience. I learned how to sell my ideas through trial and error, frustration and disillusionment. Ultimately, I learned how to do it. It was quite a trip. It wasn't at all what I expected. It wasn't what is taught in most business schools, because as helpful as business schools might be, there is a difference between theory and actual practice. Several schools have realized this and have asked me to bring what I know and share it with their graduate students. They found what I had to say worthwhile, and generally a number of people would buttonhole me after a lecture to ask far more specific questions than I could answer in a two-hour presentation. Many of them also asked if I would put my experience down in book form, in more detail. So, after all this prodding, I did. It is my fond hope that my experience selling patented concepts and new products can help you succeed with yours as well. What worked for me will probably work for you.

There is not a lot of theory here because this book isn't theoretical in the slightest. It is my experience as I lived it. It is what I found as I sold products. I imagine you will find many of the same things still exist as you go down your own particular road toward selling your idea. The only difference is that now they won't come as a surprise to you.

This book will walk you through each phase, sometimes with blow-by-blow descriptions. It should save you the toil and trouble I had to endure going nose-to-nose with company executives and lawyers who had a lot more experience than I did when I first got started. *How to Sell Your Idea* is designed to give you some practical advice and a description of what you are going to face, and to help you deal with it.

Boy... where, oh, where was this book thirty years ago?

So, what I will share with you in this book is not what you'd like to find or what you imagine you'll find when you set out to sell your idea; instead, it is what you will actually find. I know, because I've been there. I know, because I've done it – time and again. You can, too.

Before we begin, there is something you should know (and they won't tell you this in all those other books): If you have a great idea, swell. But I have found that it's not enough to come up with a great idea. It's not enough even to perfect that idea. That's just the beginning. The most important task you face is to bring that idea to market and get full value for it.

Right now, all you have is a good idea. You are really proud of it. You're excited about the possibilities. That's great!

But have you ever thought, Is it salable?

How do you know? How do you analyze what you have and find out who to take it to? It might work, but so what? Does that mean someone will pay you for it?

You might be surprised to find that most good ideas aren't worth the paper they were sketched out on. As a matter of fact, most ideas that are covered by patents never make enough to pay for the cost of getting the patent in the first place.

Wouldn't it be handy to know what chance your idea has of making any money, before you rush right down to your local patent attorney and start writing checks?

If you are certain that your idea is good enough to protect, then what kind of protection do you really need? Maybe you don't need a patent at all, or maybe you can't patent what you have in the first place. How do you know?

Finally, even with patent in hand on a product that you are convinced is salable, how do you present your idea to a potential customer in the most eye-catching way possible so they will want to buy it? You aren't the only person with good ideas. There are all kinds of other inventors with good ideas, and they want the very same thing that you do. Just like you, they want to get their idea to market. So, what is it going to take to catch a customer's eye, to convince someone that your idea is worth producing and selling? What's the trick to getting it onto the shelf?

At first, it might seem that the best way would be to just turn the idea over to some lawyer or marketing guru and let them sell it for you. Just hire the expertise. That idea occurred to me, too. But then I thought, "Wait a minute. I can always give it to someone else later. Why not try to do it myself first?" I realized I could always fall back on that approach.

If, after reading this book and trying to do it yourself you find that you aren't successful, what's the harm? You've wasted some time, sure. But you also learned a lot – and you still have all the same options that you have right now. You can always hire lawyers and marketing gurus or whatever it takes to help you get your idea sold. But don't you owe it to yourself (and to your bank account) to find out whether you can learn how to sell your idea to someone without all that expensive assistance?

As it turns out, I didn't need a lawyer or a marketing guru to sell my ideas. I was able to do it myself. And after realizing that, I found a great side benefit: After I did it once, I found I could do it again and again. You can too. If you came up with one good idea, you probably have quite a few inside you. Once you learn how to sell your first idea, you can go back to the well of ideas inside of yourself and do it again and again.

You're very lucky, you know. Some people can't do what you have already done. They have great difficulty creating new ideas, products, and inventions. But you have a unique ability. Doesn't it make sense to put that talent to work to help not only yourself but also your family and perhaps the entire world?

Now, you can learn like I did... by falling on your face a number of times and dusting yourself off and repeating the process again and again until you get it right. Or you can benefit from the experience I gathered (with all the bruised feelings and painful lessons) and start with a lot of that knowledge already under your belt. It's your choice.

I believe you'll find this book useful, and I've tried to make it easy. To accomplish that I've divided the entire process into several parts. Each part is important, but depending on your particular situation, some parts will be of more value to you than others. It can't be helped. I've written this book to help just about anyone with an idea to sell. At times I have to be pretty general so everyone will benefit. Then, at other times, I will go into a lot more detail. You'll have to judge for yourself where you are in the mix.

For example, if you work for a company that has patent attorneys or contract specialists, then a lot of the material in the sections on patents and contracts won't be as helpful as it might be for the single entrepreneur who has this terrific hill to climb and feels all alone. Depending on your idea and your previous experience, you will find value in different sections. But no matter who you are or what situation you find yourself in, you've at least got this book to tell you what to expect.

The book is structured as follows:

- Part I, "Evaluating Your Idea," covers just what it says: how to decide whether your idea is a good one. Good ideas are valuable, and you might be the person who has one of those ideas that will improve not only your life but also society as a whole. I wish I could tell you that the old saying about the world beating a path to your door to buy that better mousetrap is actually true. But in all my years no one has ever come knocking at my door. It just has never happened to me. As a matter of fact, I don't know of any inventor who just sat back and then one day found their idea sold without putting some work into it.

So, if you are going to have to sell your idea, you need to know how the business works. You need to begin with realistic expectations, and that's what this first section will deal with. After all, having a great idea is not the same as getting it to market, and as we shall see, getting that done is a lot more difficult than thinking about getting it done. So this section homes in on the single most important aspect of an idea – its salability. This part should save you lots of time and lots of money. It will keep you from wasting both on ideas that just won't go anywhere. There are good, solid reasons why inventions succeed, and there are good, solid reasons why they don't. I want to make sure that you know those reasons and concentrate only on the ideas that will do you some good.

Inventions or ideas without a good market are thought up all the time. I come up with bunches just like bananas. But over the years I've learned that every banana doesn't have to be picked. Some need to remain on the tree until it's time for picking, and some shouldn't be picked at all!

There is more to successfully selling your idea than the idea itself. There are a lot of conditions outside of your own eagerness to take your idea to market that can influence its acceptability. This section will help you determine what some of those influences might be. These principles can help you tell whether you have a really ripe banana here or one that could just waste your time and make you slip and fall.

- Part II, "Protecting Your Idea," spells out the steps
  both small and large that are essential to ensuring legal
  ownership of your idea. There are times in getting your
  idea to market where you'll have some questions to answer. When do you get a patent? When do you not need
  one? When should you hire someone else to do the marketing or the advertising or whatever?

As you've probably noticed, over the years, an industry of hucksters has grown up that preys on every inventor's very natural human desire to let someone else do
what seems new and difficult. It drives me crazy when I
hear about inventors who have fallen for some of these
shysters. All I can tell you is what happened to me. Getting your idea sold doesn't take any special talent; it
doesn't require an academic degree or fabulous connections. There is no one out there who can sell your idea
better than you can. But there are lots of people who
want to convince you that the whole process is way beyond you and your skills, and that you need to hire them
to do it for you. Don't believe it. You can do this. I did,
and I bet you can too.

On the other hand, one area where you don't want to
take chances is in arranging for protection for your
great idea. That very possibly will require professional
help. You have to be careful determining the type of protection you need for your particular idea. As you will see,
the kind of protection you need depends on the kind of
product you have. Sometimes a patent isn't even needed
or desirable.

If you determine that your particular product needs a
patent, then you need to know a bit about what kind of
patents you can get and what patents include in the first
place. Once again, when it comes to obtaining patent

protection, there are dangerous scams out there that can ensnare you, so you need to have a little help. Not every patent is a good one, and some are downright useless.

However, besides protection, a patent can be useful in generating interest in your product. You probably never thought of that, did you? Obtaining protection gives you bargaining power. It gives you something to sell. Not getting protection for your idea gives you nothing, but it does give someone else something. If your idea is a good one, you might just have made it easy for someone else to steal it. So it pays to be careful and to understand the ground rules of this whole patent-acquisition process.

Surprisingly, less than 2 percent of patents ever make back the money it costs to file for them. That's a pretty lousy batting average. We want to make sure you aren't one of the many inventors who wind up swinging at empty air and has nothing to show for their effort.

Therefore, this section is designed to give you just enough to keep you from falling into some of the larger holes and not so much that you fall asleep while you're reading.

- Part III, "Presenting Your Idea," contains tools and insights that will be valuable to anyone who has to sell something to someone. You don't have to be an inventor to benefit from this section. No matter your line of work, you will find ideas and tools in this section that you can't find anywhere else. I know – I tried to find them, and they're just not there.

Over the years, however, I began to notice what works and what doesn't, and that's what you'll find in this section. If you're going to successfully get your product on the shelf, you are going to need some of these tools available. Let's face it, you are going to be going into battle, and you'd better know what is going to be needed and make sure you are properly armed and ready.

- Part IV, "Profiting from Your Idea," takes you into the endgame, where you get to finally seal the deal. Frankly, a lot of good ideas have been ruined by bad deals. There are a lot of ways to make that idea of yours earn you money, but there also are a lot of very sharp business executives who are used to eating inexperienced inventors for breakfast. We don't want that happening to you. You want the best deal you can get, one that's fair to you and fair to your customer. You don't want these folks taking advantage of you.

  The chapters in Part IV will help. These chapters will show you how to get what your idea is worth and how to squeeze as much compensation as you can from your creativity. After all, you're the person who thought it up and made it work. It would be a pity to let the lawyers and executives who have inked lots and lots of deals with inventors take advantage of you. You're new to the game and at a terrible disadvantage. This book will help level the playing field.

As you can see, *How to Sell Your Idea* is a practical book. It's written for serious people with good ideas to bring to market. You deserve the best I can give you. I hope this book will help you get your idea refined, protected, and sold with the best possible deal. That's why I wrote it.

One final note: As you go through this process and meet with success (and I honestly believe you will), I'd like you to tell me about it. Send me an e-mail at www.howtosellyouridea .com. or www.stuartjkamille.com. Either way, you'll reach me. If you don't want me to share your experience with others, just say so and I'll honor your request. If you indicate that you won't mind if others learn from your experience, then I'll put it to good use.

Dreaming up an idea can be pretty exciting. Getting paid for it can be a real journey. It is going to be a lot easier with this book by your side, but it still is going to take some effort to hear that cash register ringing at the end of the rainbow. At the end of the day, it's up to you. Your idea won't sell itself; you're the one who has to decide to take the plunge.

That's really why I went to the trouble to write this book in the first place. Ideas are important, and I'd like to know that I helped someone else get a great idea into the marketplace.

I sure hope that "someone" is you!

PART I

Evaluating Your Idea

CHAPTER 1

Taking Your Idea from Dream to Reality

O ne of the richest men in the world today, Bill Gates, made his money at a young age. Every year, he just keeps getting wealthier. By some estimates, Mr. Gates is now worth around $56 billion. How did he make his money? He had a good idea and he made the most of it.

In 1975, he and his boyhood friend, Paul Allen, formed a software development company called Microsoft. Today, Microsoft has nearly sixty thousand employees and offices around the world. Why is his company so successful? Mr. Gates invented something the world is willing to pay him a lot of money for. So can you.

You don't have to have an extensive education or be an expert to invent a wildly successful product. As a matter of fact, most really successful products are easily understood, and the need for them is immediately obvious when their use is pointed out. But sometimes a new product just drops out of the sky. Here you are, trying to figure out how to do something better, and suddenly you find you are going in an entirely different direction.

Take the story of Spencer Silver, who in 1970 was a company chemist working on various kinds of adhesive. One day, he found that he had succeeded in developing a new adhesive. The trouble was that it was weaker than any other adhesive already on the market. One of the attributes of his new glue was that although the adhesive would stick to just about any surface, it also could be easily picked up without leaving any residue.

Silver was stumped. Who would want an adhesive that didn't stick very well? He asked around at work, and no one knew what possible application this nonstick stickum could have. No one knew what to do with the stuff.

As it happened, one of Silver's colleagues, Arthur Fry, sang in a church choir and marked songs in his hymnal with little pieces of paper. Unfortunately, the little pieces of paper were constantly falling out, and Arthur kept losing his place. Then, in a flash of inspiration, he remembered the stickum that Spencer Silver had developed. Fry put some on the back of his hymnal markers and was quite pleased. The weak adhesive held his little pieces of paper in place but didn't leave any residue in the hymnal. It was just the stuff for marking things with a paper tag and then being able to remove the tags without damage.

As it turns out, both Silver and Fry worked for Minnesota Mining and Manufacturing Company – 3M – the same folks who make miles and miles of cellophane tape. When the two men explained the use for Silver's special nonstick glue, company executives decided to distribute a test batch to their office staff. What a surprise! Secretaries began using it to flag important papers; executives began jotting down phone numbers and sticking them to their telephones. The little flags were really useful. So, in 1980, 3M started national distribution of these familiar and useful little items under the registered trademark name Post-it. You probably use them every day.

You may be thinking to yourself that you have to be a chemist or an electronics whiz to actually make something that the world will want and, more importantly, will be willing to pay you for. Certainly, having training is important; but often, inspired ideas spring into people's minds for no apparent reason.

A case in point is one Albert J. Parkhouse, who in 1903 was employed by the Timberlake Wire and Novelty Company in Jackson, Michigan. This manufacturer specialized in lampshade frames and other items made from wire. One particularly blustery day, Parkhouse arrived at work to find that all the hooks for hanging coats were already taken. Now this was frustrating. Where could he hang his hat and coat? Parkhouse took one of the pieces of spare wire that were always lying about the place and bent it in opposite directions, then tied the ends together by twisting the wire – and thereby invented the wire coat hanger. Useful? Undoubtedly. Simple? Absolutely. Valuable? Well, it was valuable to his company's owners, who took out a patent on their employee's idea and made a fortune. Parkhouse, however, didn't get a dime for it.

So here we have three hugely successful ideas that range from highly technical software to chemistry to plain, old-fashioned ingenuity. All were great ideas, and you could come up with just that sort of idea yourself. Perhaps you already have. But, as it turns out, coming up with an idea is the easiest part of getting an invention to market. What should you do with your great idea, once you have it? Where do you take it? How do you find out how good it is? How much of your own money should you put into it? And once you have a customer, how do you get the best deal for yourself?

These are the subjects of the chapters ahead.

If you work for a big company such as 3M and use its facilities to develop your idea, chances are your idea belongs to the company. The company is paying you, and you pay it back by giving it your work. Actually, this can be very helpful. Large corporations such as 3M have countless patents and a huge staff of lawyers, marketing people, and production people who can take your simple little idea and make a product out of it. Much of the work of getting it made and distributed and patented will be done by someone else. You came up with the idea and the rest will be done by the rest of your company. However, keep in mind that the more you let other people do for you, the less value you will extract from your idea.

In general, large companies won't neglect an employee who comes up with a great idea. You will probably get a raise and certainly will earn a lot of notice from upper management, which might help you in the future. You might even get a promotion. It's a win-win situation.

But what if you don't work for a big company that has all that support? What then? It would be nice if you knew someone in a big company who might think your idea was a good one, wouldn't it?

That's what happened to a simple tailor in Reno, Nevada, named Jacob Davis. Davis had tried a variety of occupations – miner, sailor, store owner – and failed at every one. But one thing he had learned as a child was tailoring, and he could always fall back on that. During the days of the great nineteenth-century silver and gold bonanza in Virginia City, Nevada, miners needed durable pants that would allow them to hang their hammers and spikes from the pockets and keep their hands free. Davis started making pants from the duck material he purchased from the wholesale house of Levi Strauss & Co., in San Francisco. His pants were sturdy, but he wanted a way to make them even sturdier for the rough mining trade. Finally, he decided to put rivets at the points of maximum stress, such as the pocket corners and the base of the button fly.

Davis's pants were a great success, and soon he had more orders than he could fill. But the idea of riveting pants could be imitated by anyone, so he decided he needed the protection of a large company. Davis realized he didn't have the means or know-how to produce these pants on a large scale. The time had come for him to bring in a partner. And who better than his chief cloth supplier? He decided to write Levi Strauss & Co. a letter.

As with many immigrants in those days, English wasn't Davis's first language and naturally he couldn't write in English well. He had to dictate his letter to one of his few acquaintances in town who could write; however, as you will see, even people who could write weren't always the best spellers. So try to decipher as well as you can what Davis was saying:

Reno, July 5th, 1872
Mess. Levi Strauss & Co.

Gents,

Inclosed please find Chack for $350.00 for which please give me credit balince my account and wright me how much thare is left to my credit, deduct $4. for the Plush and Thread which I have sent back. The reason I send you so much money is because I have no use for it here and you may alowe me Interest as well as the Baink.

I also send you by Express 2 ps. Overall as you will see one Blue and one made of the 10 oz Duck which I have bought a greate many Peces of you, and have made it up to the Pants, such as the sample the secratt of them

Pants is the Rivits that I put in those Pockots and I
found the demand so large that I cannot make them fast
enough. I charge for the Duck $3.00 and the Blue $2.50
a pear. My nabors are getting yealouse of these success
and unless I secure it by Patent Papers it will soon become to be a general thing everybody will make them up
and thare will be no money in it. tharefor Gentlemen I
wish to make you a Proposition that you should take out
the Latters Patent in my name as I am the Inventor of it,
the expense of it will be about $68, all complit and for
these $68 I will give you half the right to sell all such
Clothing Revited according to the Patent, for all the
Pacific States and Teroterous the balance of the United
States and of the Pecific Coast I reserve for myself, the
investment for you is but a trifle compaired with the improvement in all Coarse Clothing. I use it in all Blankit
Clothing such as Coats, Vests and Pents, you will find it
a very salable article at a much advenst rate. Should you
decline to spent the amount required for the Patent Papers please wright to me and I will take them out at my
own expense, under all cercomestance please dont
showe the pents to anybody I have allready obtained
through Dewey & Co. of the Centific Press 2 Patents and
one was rejected, but I am so situated with a large Family that I cannot do anything with it at Present tharefore
as I have said if you wish to take out the Papers, Please
go to Dewey & Co. of the Centrific Press and have the
Papers made out in my name for 17 years they will send
them up to me for Signature. Please answer these as
soon as possible, these looks like a trifle hardley worth
speakeing off But nevertheless I knew you can make up
pents the way I do you can sell Duck Pents such as the

Sample a $30 per doz. and they will readyly retail for $3. a pair excuse these long latter, as I could not describe particulars in a short space, I have nothing more at present.

I remain yours Truely

J.W. Davis

The company owner agreed to partner with this simple tailor, and on May 20, 1873, the two men – Jacob Davis and Levi Strauss – received patent number 139,121 from the United States Patent and Trademark Office. The folks at Levi Strauss consider that day the official birthday of blue jeans. Davis was brought to San Francisco and given the job of plant manager. For the next fifty years, he had a job overseeing the manufacturing of the famous Levi's jeans that are still so popular nearly fourteen decades later. He retired from the company in the 1920s.

Pretty good job security, wouldn't you say?

So, is that something that you should do? It might be. But if you want something larger than a steady job as an inventor employed by a company, there is another way, and that's what we'll discuss in this book.

Everyone has ideas. The world is full of clever people with clever ideas. All inventions start with a dream or an idea. Dreaming is creative thinking, and it's critical to the invention process. But if that's all that's done with the idea, it will never see the light of day. It will never become a product. It will never be sold. No one will ever make a slim dime out of it. And the idea, as wonderful as it was, will flicker away and disappear like a candle flame at the end of a birthday party.

A product is an idea that has been brought to fruition. It

works. Bill Gates didn't just think about forming a company called Microsoft, he actually did it. He didn't just think about writing software, he actually did it. But he didn't stop there. After he wrote the software, he sold it to IBM and soon to the entire world. Selling an idea is what we deal with here: taking your idea from the concept stage and making it into something that someone can buy. It is about taking your idea and making it real. The dreaming stops here. From here on, your idea is going to become reality.

So, here's your first dose of the reality of selling your really great idea: Just because you have an idea doesn't necessarily mean it is going to be worth putting enough time and money into it to make it into a product.

How do you find out? Here's how I go about it.

To figure out if I have a chance of selling an invention or product I:

- Evaluate what the product is and where potential buyers for that product are.
- Determine what it is about the invention that makes it different from other products in the field.
- Determine whether I can find some way to protect or demonstrate my ownership of the product.
- Present the product to a buyer and reach an agreement that is fair to me and to the buyer.

To sell your invention or product, I think you should look at it in the same way. What happens if you just pick up the phone and call Home Depot and tell them you have this great widget you want to sell them? In my experience, not much. That's just not the way the game is played. Selling your idea is a business, and if you don't put some effort into doing it correctly, something is going to go wrong. You will not be able to receive anything for your idea, and it very possibly will slip from your hands and become valueless.

All inventors love their idea and think it is just about the most precious thing on earth. They often love their idea so much and think their particular widget is so downright clever and desirable that it is going to walk out the front door and sell itself to everyone down the street.

Well, I think you realize that if you want to sell this idea you have to be realistic. Several myths and a lot of half-truths have accumulated around the idea of making big bucks out of your idea, but there's nothing mystical about it. It's a business, pure and simple, done by businesspeople who generally act in a businesslike way.

Yes, you can make big bucks. Yes, you can invent something that will allow you to retire and live the rest of your life in luxury. But most of the time a clever idea is just that – a clever idea. It's not going to be something the world just can't do without. Often, it's not a thing at all. Perhaps it's just an improved way of doing something. Improvements to a process that lower costs or improve efficiency are real inventions that make real people real money. You don't have to invent a perpetual motion machine to make money from your idea. On the other hand, many inventive people who figure out a little twist on someone else's basic idea often get the misguided notion that their little idea is more valuable than the Hope diamond.

The truth is that most ideas aren't that valuable. I'm sorry to say it, but most ideas are only moderately valuable. These ideas can make you money, but don't expect them to pay off your mortgage, send your kids to college, and buy you a new red sports car. Getting paid for your ideas is a business, just like any other business. If you ask too much for your product, it's going to be hard to sell to someone. If you ask too little, you aren't going to make much from it. So let's be realistic in our expectations.

Your idea probably isn't going to require armed guards and a secret laboratory. It probably isn't going to revolutionize an industry. But if you find that it does have value, it can make you a steady income. If it's patentable and popular, that income stream can go on for up to twenty years. So it's worth the effort.

Look at it this way: With a string of good little products working for you, you're in a great position. You can send your ideas out to make money for you just like the seven dwarfs going off to the diamond mine. Every day another little check arrives. Perhaps your idea isn't as valuable as diamonds, but if you're collecting checks and not doing much more than singing an occasional "Hi Ho, Hi Ho," what's so terrible about that?

With that in mind, let's take a look at that idea of yours and determine whether it's worth going through all the steps outlined in this book. Don't be surprised if somewhere in the process you suddenly realize that there are some large holes in your idea. Perhaps it's a great idea but not protectable. Perhaps it's protectable but not salable. Perhaps it really isn't an invention at all. Any of these reasons should cause you to pause and reflect.

As a matter of fact, I'll go even further. If your idea has any of these failings, then *stop*. These failings are real deal killers. If you can't fix the problem, you would be well advised to drop the idea and go on to something else. I realize that this advice might cause you some short-term pain, but it will save you many wasted hours and a lot of heartbreak.

Selling ideas is not simply a case of perseverance. Belief in your idea is one thing, but downright stubborn neglect of serious problems is another. Your idea is only as good as its salability. It might be clever, but clever ideas are cheap. Good ideas that someone will buy are valuable. Which do you have?

CHAPTER 2

What Have You Got Here, Anyway?

You may think you have a really clever idea. Your mother and your father and your pet cat might agree. But the truth is that they aren't the people who are going to produce your idea or buy it. For that, you need an established company. This ideal company is going to be made up of businesspeople who make items such as yours every day. They know the business. They deal with all the difficulties and peculiarities of this business every day.

Here you eagerly come with your widget tucked under your arm. What kind of reception do you imagine you will get? That first impression is very important. I can guarantee that they will all greet you with the same expectation: They will expect you to understand their business as well as they do. This could be a big problem, because they deal with this business every day and you don't. Doesn't it just make sense that you are going to be at a disadvantage? We can't have that. So, this is what you should do.

Before you make any appointment to present any idea, do some homework. Initially, you'll need to get a handle on the size of the market, the customer's market share, what the potential market is, and who their competition is. Why? Because that's what businesspeople think about.

Put yourself in their place. If someone came to you and asked you to buy a new product that they had come up with, what would you want to know about it? How big a new market is this? What is the potential for this idea? What's in it for us? It's that simple.

Now, you might ask, If they know this business so well, won't they know how big the market is? Won't they realize what's in it for them? Why should I tell them something they already know?

You should realize that you are up against experts, all right, but they're also expert specialists. Each has a specific job. Their company is divided into different departments. The folks in marketing will certainly understand the size of the market, but they won't have a clue how difficult your idea will be to make or ship, or how much it's going to cost to get it into the hands of a customer. The folks in sales won't have any idea where the raw material might come from or the labor to assemble it. The folks in production don't have to sell it, so they won't give a second thought to what benefits the product might provide. You are the only person who has all those threads in your hands at the same time.

You are going to be in a meeting at some point with all these experts, each representing their specialty, and they will be asking you questions about your product from their own unique point of view. They have every right to expect that you are going to know the answers to those specific questions, because you are asking them to buy your product!

This means you need to get all this information before you walk into the conference room. Once you are standing there with all these experts asking you questions, it is too late. You are going to get one shot at this, so make it your best.

Next, you need to prepare your presentation so that all this information is presented in a clear and memorable way. Many new inventors with little experience make the fundamental mistake of assuming that their wonderful idea will practically sell itself. They mistakenly think that their idea is just so darn clever that anyone could understand it right away. But the truth is, most customers won't understand it right away. If it were so obvious that they would see it right away... they would already have thought of it and you wouldn't have any reason to be standing there in the first place. So you will need to help them "get it." All these people must be sold.

If you have managed to get someone interested in your idea, they deserve an organized and businesslike presentation. They are running a business. They have lots to do. Listening to your clever idea isn't the only thing they are going to do today. Do you really think that you are going to get their attention if you haven't thought your idea through and know where it fits into their business? Why should they put any effort into selling themselves your idea? That's why you are standing there. It's your job, not theirs.

At first, you are actually just a nuisance and a potential problem. The last thing they want is to waste their time with someone who doesn't understand their business, who doesn't understand the potential of the idea or how much money can be made from it, or who doesn't know anything at all about how to build the product, distribute it, or sell it. If your idea has value and you can make it clear to them how valuable it is right away, I guarantee their attitude will change. Instead of a nuisance, you will become a valuable asset. But that won't happen until you get them to see things your way.

They won't expect you to understand all the intricacies of their business – after all, it is their business. Chances are, a lot of the information they might want isn't going to be available to you. For example, you aren't going to know what their markup is or details about their distributorships. But they will. After you leave, there will be meetings to analyze your product, and that is when all this important internal information will get plugged into their calculations. But even if you don't have all the specifics, you should still have a general idea of how your idea will fit into their company. You need to demonstrate that you have a pretty good idea where this product fits and what it will take to bring it to market. They will be able to take it from there.

The best way to demonstrate your understanding is to present the relevant facts in a concise, clear, and logical way. That concise, clear, and logical way is called a business plan.

Now, don't freeze up with fear. Writing a business plan doesn't take a college degree or an MBA or even much experience with business. A business plan is simply a summary of all the facts that you have gathered about the production, sales potential, and market appeal of your product. It's a script that you can work from. It is going to keep you from stumbling through this very critical material, confusing your audience, and embarrassing yourself.

Look at it this way: If you have a good idea, then treat it that way. Give it the respect it deserves. If you don't respect it, why should a potential client?

A business plan will help you sell your idea because it will build interest in your idea. You use the business plan to show the customer that you know what you are doing and are not going to waste their time. Rule number one in any business is not to waste time. There is never enough time to do everything that has to be done. You and your idea could be a terrific benefit to them, but from their point of view, it also could be a terrific waste of time. If you impress them that you know what you are dealing with, you will have their respect and their complete and undivided attention.

The nice part about your business plan is that it isn't really all that difficult to write. We shall deal with business plans and preparation of your presentation later.

CHAPTER 3

What Every Product Must Provide

If you have never evaluated an idea before, you need to be aware of some basic business fundamentals that every product must take into account. These are important to any company because they can stop any product dead in its tracks. If you haven't considered these, you are bound to fail. They are critically important to the salability of the product. They are:

- market sensitivities,
- return on investment,
- cannibalism, and
- impact on the industry.

Market Sensitivities

Industries often have information and quirks that only people close to the business really appreciate. These quirks and insights are only picked up after years of experience, and over time they become ingrained in the way a company will look at any new product. If you lack that perspective, it is going to show up right away, and it can hurt you. Therefore, if your idea is in a field that you don't know a lot about, it's in your best interest to get close to someone in that field and get some advice before you wade into their little pond with your invention held high above your head. A little insight from an old hand right at the beginning can give you that business's perspective, and when you are making your presentation, your knowledge of that perspective can keep you from ending up all wet. Let me give you an example.

Over the years, I've heard a story about the new product launch of the first cake mix. I've never been able to verify that the story is actually true, but whether it's true or not, it perfectly illustrates the kind of industry peculiarity you must be aware of.

If you go to your kitchen cupboard and take out just about any brand of cake mix, you will find that the instructions on the box require you to add an egg and vegetable oil or something like that. Now, isn't that a little silly? Certainly a company that can put all the components of a cake mix together could easily add powdered egg, as well. So why don't they?

The answer is surprising, especially when you consider that it has nothing to do with how good the cake tastes. When it was originally introduced, cake mix didn't sell very well. In those days, a homemaker was judged by the quality of her cake. If she was a good cake maker, she was probably also a good homemaker. Being able to actually make a good cake – from scratch – was important.

Baking is also a very personal and creative outlet. We all have heard Pillsbury's famous advertising line, "Nothin' says lovin' like somethin' from the oven." So baking a good cake has a lot of emotional energy tied up in it. It's easy to see: As soon as a piece of cake is served, everyone says, "Oh, what a wonderful cake *you* baked."

And that explains why early cake mixes didn't sell very well. After all, if all you actually do is rip off the top of the box, pour the contents into a pan, and bake it, where's the personal creativity? The homemaker didn't actually *bake* the cake, so the baker was no longer involved, and the boxed cake mix didn't sell.

What's a cake-mix company to do? The answer was very simple: Leave something out so the baker can add it at home. The cake-mix company left out a simple ingredient like an egg, just to make sure that the baker felt involved. And guess what? Sales took off.

Why? It's certainly not as efficient. The additional cost of adding the "missing" ingredient wasn't substantial, so that wasn't it. This is simply understanding the market. If you do this every day, you pick up this knowledge. If you aren't a regular in the business, it will blow right by you. And that leads to a lot of hurt feelings.

This is why the inventor of a new cake mix might run into trouble if he approaches a cake-mix company and hasn't talked with an insider first. Here comes our hapless inventor with an absolutely jim-dandy cake mix where all you have to do is plunk the box right in the oven. Why, you don't even have to open the box! Just plunk it in the oven and fifteen minutes later out comes a complete birthday cake with fifteen candles on it, already lit. What a great idea! Could you blame our hapless inventor for being thrilled with his idea? Could you blame his family for dreaming about yachts and islands in the Bahamas?

What Mr. Hapless doesn't realize, though, is that no one can sell a box of cake mix that is complete right off the shelf. It's not in the nature of the business. So how far do you think this absolutely great idea will get with the bakers of the world? See what I mean? Mr. Hapless is going to be turned down flat – even though it's a terrific idea.

This is why so many inventors have the feeling that there is a conspiracy to keep good ideas off the market. If you ask Mr. Hapless why his really great idea didn't get to first base, he'll tell you that there is an industry conspiracy going on. Company after company threw him out on his ear. The world is against him. They aren't being reasonable. They don't want new ideas. They're jealous. They are all infected with the "not invented here" syndrome.

But is that what really is going on? I'm not saying that the not invented here syndrome doesn't exist, but often there is a much less sinister explanation. What looks like jealousy is just the inventor's lack of appreciation of the fundamentals of that particular business.

Knowing what we now know about the prevalent outlook of the cake mix biz, we can see that it wasn't that Mr. Hapless's idea wasn't any good. It was his lack of industry understanding. He didn't do his homework. And because he didn't do his homework, he got what he deserved.

Every business has its own viewpoint and it's up to you to know about it. You must be sensitive to what your particular market needs and expects.

Sometimes great ideas can't be adopted because they fly in the face of convention and are just too far a stretch. What food company would ask a homemaker to throw a dirty box that just came out of the warehouse into the oven and eat it? Now, you could argue that the baking would sterilize the cake – but would customers agree? Would you want to be the company that offered that product to the homemakers of America? What do you think it would do to the company's reputation? What would everyone think of the guy who approved the idea when it first showed up? Yet, there is no denying it's a wonderful idea.

Return on Investment

Market sensitivity like the attitude of the cake-mix company is one of several general factors that you must take into consideration before arranging for patents, contracts, meetings, and so on. Return on investment is another.

Did you know that even though the railroad (the Baltimore & Ohio) was introduced in the United States in 1827, the railroad gauge (the width between the rails) wasn't standardized in the nation until 1886, when the Southern and Northern railroad companies agreed on a standard width? For sixty years, railroad carriages had to be unloaded at the end of one line and reloaded onto another in order to continue the trip. This was inefficient, slow, and cumbersome, but the different gauges protected each railroad's business. Why?

Each railroad required a lot of investment by its owners. By maintaining a different gauge for their lines, railroads were able to lock in their particular market. Once a standard gauge was introduced, that advantage was lost. It took sixty years before enough railroads were satisfied that the benefits of a standard gauge would surpass that of a guaranteed market.

The lesson to learn here is to be mindful of what you are asking of your potential customer. Companies might have a very good reason not to want to change to make room for your idea, especially if the idea is going to risk changing their relationship with their present market. They might be in the same place as the railroad companies of the 1800s and want to recover the cost of their initial investment before introducing a new idea that will change the basic way they do business. It's not that the idea isn't great; it's just that it's coming to them at the wrong time or that the game isn't worth the candle. This happens all the time. Good ideas get turned down just because they are going to cost too much. They demand too much. It has nothing to do with how good the idea is. It has everything to do with how much your idea is going to require from the customer.

Here's a way to get a handle on that. Look at your product as if you were the client. If you were the CEO of this company, what would you want to know about this product? Wouldn't you want to know what is going to be required to manufacture and introduce this new widget or whatever? Is it going to require a new manufacturing method or a really large change in the way you usually do business? Is it going to require a large investment, like the B&O in 1827?

Let's say the idea has really great potential, just like the railroad, but is going to cost a lot to get off the ground. Where do you find the money? If you can find the money, how long will it take to get the product out the door? What's the risk of raising that much money compared to how much you might be able to make? Can you keep control of this product, keep it out of the hands of the competition, and carve out a large chunk of a new, profitable market?

Now, these are all CEO types of questions, and perhaps your idea doesn't fall into the industry-changing kind of category. Still, just because your idea won't cost as much as a railroad doesn't mean that everyone who looks at your product won't think the same thing: Your product, as modest as it may seem to be, is going to cost someone something. Is that cost, no matter how small, worth the amount of profit the company will make? The return on investment is the single most important element in getting a company to purchase your idea. So what does that mean to you?

It should be clear that you must make the return on investment a very high priority item in your presentation. You must be sure to show that the investment they might make in your product will be worth it. That value can be as little as a new way to do something that will cut costs or as large as an entirely new way to use their equipment that will return a handsome profit. Either way, the benefit must be worth the investment.

And don't assume that benefit is going to be obvious. It's your job to make sure they see it. If you don't point it out to them, chances are that no one else will.

This fundamental characteristic is true of every product: It must be worth the investment. Whatever it is that you are asking someone to buy must return a significant benefit that outweighs the investment they will need to make.

A number of years ago I consulted with a food company that had developed a really wonderful snack food. They had a product that scored way off the charts when consumers tasted it. It wasn't expensive and it was very stable, so freshness wouldn't be a problem. The potential market was huge because the product was ideal for selling in vending machines. There was just one hitch: It couldn't be put into a package that would fit the standard vending machine.

See the problem? To sell this great idea, we would have to ask all the folks who owned vending machines to buy new machines. From their perspective, the price of offering this wonderful new product wasn't just in buying the product – they also had to buy new vending machines. Guess what? The idea was quietly put aside and never saw the light of day. Even though it would have sold like ice cubes in the Sahara, the potential volume couldn't justify the high entry cost to get the product to market.

Do you have a product like that? Is it going to require a large shift in your customer's usual business? If it does, look out. You have a steep climb and a rutty road to follow.

Cannibalism

Did you realize that a new invention can devour an older one? As a matter of fact, most new inventions have the capacity to hurt a company as much as help it. That's because inventions and improvements don't necessarily add anything to a company's business. In fact, inventions have the capacity to bleed sales from a current product and leave the company with no net gain at all.

Here's what I mean: Let's say you have developed a new kind of laundry detergent that gets clothes 10 percent cleaner than XYZ detergent. It's a great new idea. So you rush right down to the XYZ company and you get a meeting with all the right people and you wash some clothes and prove beyond a shadow of a doubt that your soap suds are 10 percent better. No one can dispute it.

Do you know what will happen? I can tell you – I've been there. They will turn you down flat!

But why? Your product is undoubtedly better. It cleans 10 percent better and it smells good too. Are they crazy? Is there a conspiracy? Here we go again with the not invented here syndrome, right? Nope, not in the least.

They will glance knowingly at each other and then look at you with an innocent smile and ask, "Tell me, what do you think this will do to the sales of our XYZ brand of laundry detergent?"

And you will be honest and say, "Why, everyone will buy this new product. It not only cleans better, it smells good, too."

Then they are going to say something like, "Would you please tell us why we should want to ruin the sales of XYZ when we have spent millions of dollars to advertise it and develop it into a household name? Do you realize that XYZ is one of our best-selling products? Do you know how many millions of dollars XYZ contributes to our bottom line... every year? *Are you crazy?* Why should we throw out what is working so well just because your product cleans a measly 10 percent better?"

The reason XYZ company is going to turn you down is not because your product isn't terrific. Yes, it's a good product. And people would love it. They would buy boxes and boxes. And that's the problem. The people who buy boxes and boxes of your wonderful new product won't need boxes and boxes of XYZ anymore. Your product will devour all of XYZ – cannibalism.

Now, you might ask why the XYZ company should care. They aren't going to lose any money if they acquire your idea. The sales they lose from XYZ will be made up by sales of the new laundry detergent. So what's the big deal?

The big deal is that there is nothing in it for XYZ. It takes a lot of effort, time, and money to launch a new product. Your product will require a lot to get it into the hands of consumers. And the XYZ company will end up having invested all this energy and time only to end up right where they started. Their sales won't increase. They will sell the same amount of the new detergent as they did of the old detergent. But it will be less profitable because they will have spent millions getting the new product into the market. So they end up losing money, or at best breaking even.

That's what is meant by cannibalism – taking sales from one product to build up sales of another. It's the marketing equivalent of taking money from your left pocket and putting it in your right. At the end of the day, you aren't any better off, just balanced differently.

So why don't we just put our new formula in the XYZ box?

Ten percent improvement and no cannibalism, right? Who would know? The company gets an improved product and you can rush right down to buy that flashy red sports car. Good deal, right?

Nope. Sorry. A move like that also could cost the company something very valuable... the loyalty of its customers. That's because it might actually drive customers away – exactly the opposite of what you thought might happen. How can this be?

Any improvement means something is going to have to change, and change is a pretty tricky issue. The public is very sensitive to product changes, especially changes to products they really like and have been buying for years. Most inventors don't understand what it takes to get a product launched. It's difficult getting a brand established, and once a brand is established, a company is crazy to change it unless they have very compelling reasons to do so.

To show you what I mean, let's consider XYZ company's new product, New and Improved XYZ. You will remember that the new product "smelled good too." So, here we have Mr. or Ms. Houseperson. They are off to their local supermarket to pick up their trusty box of XYZ. They've been using XYZ for years. Good old XYZ cleans clothes like no other. Here they are at the soapsuds aisle. They look down the rows upon rows of laundry products. Aah, there it is... good old XYZ.

But wait.... Something new here... They see on the label, NEW AND IMPROVED FORMULA MAKES YOUR CLOTHES 10% CLEANER.

Great! Better is better, right? So they shrug and take it home. Laundry time... They open the box and–whew!– what is this new smell? It doesn't smell like the same, good old reliable XYZ. Something is amiss here. And although the smell isn't bad, it's different somehow.

And that is the kiss of death. Customers expect their product to perform in a certain way. If a change is made, even a change for the better, it's going to be very hard to convince customers that the change actually *is* better. After all, the company spent millions selling customers on the first brand. Now here you come, asking XYZ to replace all that with something that, though slightly improved, isn't going to put any extra nickels into the corporate piggy bank.

And then consider the risk. If you were the CEO of XYZ, would you want to bet the farm on the nose of all those loyal customers? For what reason? Is making the product work 10 percent better going to improve your sales by 10 percent? Probably not. People are loyal to their brand, and it would take a heck of a lot more than a little boost in brightness to make most of them switch. So here you are, taking a million-dollar gamble for a zero percent return on investment. This is just *not* going to happen. They don't teach you that in CEO school.

To show you how real this kind of a problem can be, here's something you probably witnessed yourself. Remember "new Coke"? It was tested carefully and thoroughly, and everyone who tried it really liked it. It was going to be the best new product the Coca-Cola Company had ever put out. But sales never took off. Instead, it became a rather famous marketing debacle.

So what went wrong? Nothing went wrong. Americans expected the new Coke to taste like the old Coke, and it almost did – but not quite – so consumers stayed away. This was a classic error in marketing, and it took the folks at Coca-Cola completely by surprise. Unfortunately, in their enthusiasm to introduce the new formula, they didn't consider the strength of their own brand. The original Coke was loved by millions of customers. They had a successful product. Their loyal customers didn't want a new Coke; they liked what they had. As a result, customers actually resented the new upstart. They clung even more tightly to their familiar brand. This is sort of the opposite of cannibalism. Instead of devouring the old product's customers, the old customers refused to let the new product take their favorite old product's place. I suppose you could call it consumer backlash.

Thus, cannibalism takes a variety of forms, and it isn't always just bleeding sales from one brand to a new one. If you have an idea that requires the company to replace perfectly good equipment with new equipment, and which has no other benefit, you actually aren't offering your client anything. Yes, it may be a clever new way to do what the company is already doing, but if they are doing whatever it is successfully and have already installed the equipment to do it, then why make a change in the first place?

No business is going to change just because something is new, even if it's a little bit better. It's the size of that "little bit" that makes the difference. Businesses don't stay in business by swapping dollars made with old equipment for the same number of dollars made with new equipment. Your clients want an idea that will improve their market share (increase sales) or that will reduce their cost significantly enough to warrant replacing previously purchased equipment. If your idea can do that, you might have something they are going to want.

What this means is that you have to give them a reason to want to tear up everything they have in place and do it your way. But if you can't identify a significant benefit, one that will improve their profits, increase their productivity, stream-line their distribution, or something tangible that they can't get any other way, then don't even make an appointment to present the idea to them. You don't have anything to sell.

Once again, if you asked Mr. Hapless our inventor with the great cake mix, he would swear that all these companies are filled with old fogies who never want anything new. They can't see beyond their noses. They are stuck in a rut. Have you ever heard that? It might be true sometimes, but that's probably not the explanation. Some companies are stuck in a rut, and if they continue in their rut they will soon pay for it by going out of business. In the business world, any business survives by moving forward, and that takes new ideas. Most companies want new ideas – the ideas just have to make financial and marketing sense.

Impact on the Industry

With the introduction of the diesel engine, a railroad engine could be run with one fewer employee. No one was needed to shovel the coal into the firebox and keep the steam up – diesel engines didn't burn coal. Not only was the diesel a more efficient operating system but also it was a labor saver. One would think that companies would be rushing down to the nearest diesel store and signing right up.

But it wasn't quite like that. In fact, it was just the oppo-site. Companies took their time. They knew that switching from steam engines to diesel engines was going to have a massive effect on their labor force and had the potential to generate a lot of headaches. Any development that was going to lay off a huge number of union members was hardly going to be met with cheers. It wasn't that the labor unions didn't agree that the engine was a good thing; it was the effect it was going to have on their membership that made them un-happy, and they didn't hesitate to let the companies know about it.

Another idea with great impact was the electric light. Not only was it a clean and safe improvement to people's lives but also it changed society from top to toe. Nevertheless, though the electric light was an earth-shaking improvement, it was slow to catch on. In fact, the introduction of the electric light took nearly thirty years. Why? Because the electric light was the end product of a very complex system. Edison had to invent both a lightbulb that would burn long enough to be practical and the entire system to deliver the electricity. Making that electric light work required laying down trans-mission lines and building dynamos and a whole distribution system.

Everyone agreed the idea was terrific. But even though the carbon-filament electric light was invented in 1879, it took nearly thirty years to get electricity into most U.S. homes, and it actually wasn't until the 1930s that rural America was electrified.

Lately, the marketing buzzword is *disruptive,* as in *disruptive technology.* What is meant is something so novel, so new, so different that it has the ability to impact whole industries. The diesel engine, the lightbulb, the airplane, the transistor, the Internet – they were so new they changed the world. They were disruptive. They had impact.

But impact is a very dangerous thing. If an idea is really disruptive, it can shake a company right down to its roots. People can lose their jobs, products can get swept away. Im-pact is like a forest fire or an earthquake... fascinating to watch – from far away. The very thing that is so exciting, the terrific impact of this idea, might be the very reason most companies are going to stay far, far away.

If your idea is really new, so new that no one has ever seen it before, be prepared for a more difficult time than if your idea is similar to other items. To establish a really new item, no matter how terrific it might be, requires more than just throwing it into midair and expecting that somehow, miraculously, it will find its market.

Think for a moment about how long a trip it is from the gathering of the raw materials through design, assembly, sales, production, distribution, and finally, to the shelf. Just getting a store to put the product on the shelf requires transportation, warehousing, distribution, inventory, stocking, and selling. All these steps require man- and woman-power. All require platoons of support people.

A familiar product has all of this support in place already, because there are lots of products somewhat similar to it, whereas a brand-new product has to blaze a new trail. That means a space must be created for the newcomer.

Consider your wonderful and novel widget. It has to be designed from scratch (following your plans, of course). It has to be produced, which means someone has to secure supplies and inventory the raw materials. It has to be advertised and sold to potential distributors. It has to be shipped and warehoused and stocked. And finally, the consumer has to take it off the store shelf. All of this has to be done with no pattern to follow. It's new, so there is nothing familiar to act as a guide.

Older products have to move aside to let the newcomer onto the shelf. Customers have to be told and taught what this new item is. A demand must be generated. A distribution system has to be developed.

All of that jostling for attention, reslotting, restocking, and reallocation of resources costs money, time, and people. In short, it's going to require a lot of people to go out of their way to make room for the new idea. If your idea is really disruptive, then the disruption is going to be really serious. That will cause some major upheavals.

No one can deny that the lightbulb and the transistor were worth the effort. Where would we be without them? Prior to the invention of the airplane, the fastest means of transportation was an express train – it took five days for a crack train to cross the continent from New York to Los Angeles. Now an airplane can do it in about four hours. That increase in speed has changed the entire world. Before the train, it took five months to cross the continent by wagon and ox. It took even longer to sail round Cape Horn if the weather wasn't in your favor. From five months to five days to less than five hours, all because of new, disruptive inventions.

Each new invention generated enormous wealth for its inventors and developers. Each new invention transformed its respective society. Each displaced its previous competition. Each was disruptive. For that reason, each met stiff resistance. A lot of people were put out of work or needed to be reeducated to the new product. Society had to be reeducated as well. A lot of old attitudes had to be changed. These are major undertakings, but society will do it, business will do it – if it's worth it.

Market sensitivities, the return on the company's investment, the potential for cannibalism, and the radical nature of the invention are all deal breakers. Any single one can bring your idea down, and it would have nothing to do with how clever your idea was or how well you presented it. Yet, inventors consistently forget to consider how important these factors are. They are blinded by just how clever their amazing idea is, and it never occurs to them that their amazing idea may be highly disruptive or too expensive, or that it may actually just swap dollars from one pocket to the other.

CHAPTER 4

Edison's Secret to Making Millions

We are now about to take a cold, hard look at the invention of yours, and you may be in for a shock. A cold, hard look is going to be a lot more difficult than you might think. That's because it's your invention and a part of you. It's tough to be objective.

But you must be. To succeed at selling your invention, you might want to take some advice from Thomas Alva Edison, who knew how to sell the things he had invented and who sold more than anyone else.

Edison held more than a thousand patents. He was arguably the most famous man of the nineteenth century. You use his inventions every day. He invented the phonograph, the lightbulb filament, and the electric dynamo. He developed the machinery that made motion pictures possible. He improved many products that others had invented, such as perfecting the telephone by making it more audible. Many of his inventions were hugely successful and transformed the way we live.

But it wasn't always that way. Indeed, early in his career he was headed anywhere but toward success. His first patented idea proved to be totally useless. Edison's first patent was number 90,646, an electric vote recorder. He intended to make it easier and quicker for legislatures to record the votes of their members. But there was a problem: Legislators don't want to have their votes recorded quickly. They want to take their time and be convinced that a measure is worth their votes. They want to filibuster. They want to twist arms. Just pushing a button might be efficient, but it wasn't the way lawmakers wanted to operate. Therefore, Edison never sold any of his vote recorders.

This made a deep impression on the young inventor, and it should make an impression on you. From that bitter lesson, Edison developed a motto that he lived by from then on. He made this his fundamental rule: "I find out what the world needs, then I proceed to invent."

It's very good advice. Don't waste your time on ideas that don't have a ready market. It should be a cardinal rule that every idea you consider has to have a ready and willing market.

This may seem obvious at first glance. Who would be so silly as to invent something that people wouldn't buy? The answer will amaze you: nearly every inventor. You would be astonished at the number of people who have wonderfully clever ideas that won't sell.

The trouble is that he or she is in love. Inventors fall in love with their idea. It's their baby. Their baby might have two heads, but it's beautiful to them. They will be completely blind to any of its faults. If someone points out one of these faults, the inventor immediately becomes defensive and brushes the point aside. Like a proud parent, inventors invariably believe that any obstacles in the road can easily be overcome. It will never even occur to them that perhaps these very obstacles are exactly why the idea hasn't been done before.

Young Tom Edison was in love with his vote recorder. But he learned his lesson well, and during his career his later countless "loves" were ideas that also held up under the light of withering examination.

Before you marry yourself to your idea, you must ensure that your idea is marriageable material. You must think of all the problems with it before someone else does. You might forgive yourself for not anticipating a problem, but no one else will – especially not a corporate manager sitting in your sales presentation. On the other hand, if you discover and correct the obvious flaws now, before you take your idea out on the road, you can greatly increase the value of the contract you finally sign. Think of your intense analysis as an investment in your future. You will save yourself an immeasurable amount of time and effort if you carefully and coolly evaluate the salability of your idea before you show it to the world.

But how do you proceed to do that? How do you determine whether your idea has any potential at all?

It probably has occurred to you that there are people out there who could give you advice that will help you. Most inventors will go to the people closest to the idea: a patent attorney, the patent office, friends and family, experts in the field, or perhaps a businessperson. But as we shall see, that might not be a good idea.

Patent Attorney

If you ask a patent attorney for his opinion of your idea, he will tell you that you can get a patent on it. After all, that's what he does for a living. And you can! Contrary to what you might think, patents are easy to get. You can get a patent on just about anything. So your patent attorney is telling you the absolute, unvarnished truth. He *can* get you a patent on it.

Whether this is a good idea is a much trickier question. Unless he's a very good personal friend, no patent attorney is going to give you an evaluation of your idea. If he ends up being wrong, telling you it's a great idea and then having it fall on its face, what are you going to think? He was the one giving you false hope... you could say it's his fault that you spent the money on the patent – and that will mean nothing but grief for him. What if you asked for your money back? What if you started saying that he's a lousy patent attorney – not because he didn't do what you hired him to do but because your idea wasn't salable in the first place? Now, you might not be someone who would do that, but there are lots of people who would. So he's got to be very careful.

In general, you will find that patent attorneys don't care about the salability of an idea. They care about the *patentability* of the idea. And surprisingly, patentability has nothing to do with salability... or workability... or even practicality.

U.S. Patent and Trademark Office

The U.S. Patent and Trademark Office (PTO) is in the business of granting patents to inventors. In Part II we'll be looking at patents as a way to protect your idea, but right now we will consider whether it would be a wise idea to submit your idea to the PTO for its opinion. After all, you can't get a patent on an idea that's not practical, can you?

Unfortunately, the answer is yes. Millions of patents have been issued for ideas that are completely impractical. And the truth is that many patented ideas are completely impractical and unsellable. Inventors don't like to admit it, but the PTO is not capable of helping good ideas get to market. As a matter of fact, its staff couldn't care less. That is why less than 2 percent of the more than 7 million patents granted by the PTO earn back even their original filing costs. Two percent is a mighty small figure when you think of it – .020 is a pretty poor batting average, isn't it?

The figure below is an example of one of those terrific ideas that just isn't going to work. Would you like to be the guy who literally is going to stick his neck out wearing this particular lifesaving device?

B. B. OPPENHEIMER.
Fire-Escape.
No. 221,855.   Patented Nov. 18, 1879.

WITNESSES: INVENTOR:
Henry N. Miller   B. B. Oppenheimer
C. Sedgwick   BY   Munn & Co.
                                     ATTORNEYS.

Please understand that I didn't just draw this. This is an actual U.S. patent. There are many others that I could have used. As a matter of fact, most of the patents registered by the PTO are absolutely useless, all for more or less the same reason: The person thinking it up didn't really understand what the word *doable* means.

Now do you see why the PTO can't give advice about the sales potential of your idea? Just like your patent attorney, the PTO's staff can only provide information about whether your idea is patentable. It neither cares nor has the ability to determine whether your idea is valuable.

Friends and Family

By definition, friends and family love you and are close to you. Their opinions can safely be assumed to be well intended and, if not exactly objective, at least fair. But let's face it, they don't have any more experience than you do. How are they going to know if your terrific idea is terrific?

Then there's the complication of friends and family being reluctant to tell you what you might not want to hear. After all, they're your friends and family. They may not want to say anything that might hurt your feelings, so why should you put them on the spot like that?

Now, if your uncle is an expert in aeronautics and your idea is an aeronautical one, then you have access to an expert opinion, and that's very, very good. But most of us don't have relatives like that.

This is not to say that you should not discuss your idea with your spouse or your kids or your parents. It's just that if they go into hysterical paroxysms of pure joy, take it with a grain of salt. They just aren't going to be a true measure that you can rely on.

By the way, you also should keep in mind that your family members, well meaning as they might be, will find it difficult to keep their mouths shut about this wonderful idea of yours. If a simple suggestion by your mother about how clever you are and how clever your invention is goes in the wrong ear, you might find that someone else takes your wonderful idea right away from you. We'll deal with security issues later on, but for now keep in mind that the more people you tell about your idea the more people there are who will tell other people – and who knows who they will tell. Once the genie is out of the bottle, you aren't going to get it back.

Experts

The opinion of someone who is completely familiar with the field is invaluable. It's also very hard to come by. The best person to evaluate your idea is someone who knows the field and who has no bias. Where do you find such an expert?

You won't find him or her in companies that manufacture something like your idea. These companies might have experts, but they are certainly not unbiased. If these experts told you your idea is good, your price would go up. So, more than likely, they'll tell you it isn't very good, whether it is or not.

You can hire an outside expert from a university or a business – assuming, of course, that you can find one. But besides the money it will cost you as a consulting fee, just how good will this judgment be? Let's say the expert says it's a good idea. What do you do then? You are no closer to getting it sold than you were before you hired the expert; you've just been reassured that they like it. They might be able to write you a letter of introduction to a friend or colleague, and that would be nice. But you still have to sell the idea, so the buck still stops with you.

And if your idea is really new and disruptive, then, believe it or not, experts can be poison. When it comes to a really new idea, expert opinion is usually just flat-out wrong. Experts have expert knowledge in the field as it stands now, but if your idea is an advancement in that field, they actually might end up not being an expert in the field anymore. That means they have a reputation to protect, and though they might not want to admit it, their reputation is more important to them than your idea is, and that will color their advice.

In fact, expert advice is often cited to demonstrate why your idea will never succeed. It can become a real difficulty to overcome, rather than a source of assistance in moving forward. No matter how fantastic an idea you have, no matter how superior and vastly promising the product or method is, nothing will spare you from the criticism of voices of authority within the field.

Unfortunately, you will run into these "experts" quite frequently. When you do, remember these real examples of very bad decisions made by supposedly knowledgeable professionals. In truth, they were people who just didn't want to peek over the horizon. The result, as you might imagine, was a terribly bad decision.

"These boys won't make it. Four-groups are out. Go back to Liverpool, Mr. Epstein. You have a good business there."

—*Record company executive commenting on the Beatles' first demo*

"This fellow Charles Lindbergh will never make it. He's doomed."

—*Harry Guggenheim, millionaire aviation enthusiast*

"What, sir, you would make a ship sail against the wind and currents by lighting a bonfire under her decks? I pray you excuse me. I have no time to listen to such nonsense."

—*Napoleon Bonaparte, 1803*

"What are you planning to do Mr. Bell... wire up every house in the country?"

—*Ridicule leveled at Alexander Graham Bell as he*

*presented plans for wire telephony to bankers and
investors in Philadelphia*

"Who the hell wants to hear actors talk?"

— H. M. Warner, Warner Bros., 1927

When it comes to experts and your idea, there is only one
real expert. That person is you.

Here's one final historic example of the knee-jerk resistance that innovators face, which should serve to underscore
the difficulty that novel ideas face and the obstacles that
might be placed in your way by authorities in the field with
impressive credentials.

At the dawn of the twentieth century, it was taken as a
matter of fact that humans were never going to fly. The glid-
ers at the time were so frail that they could hardly bear a
man's weight, and there seemed to be no means to lift him off
the ground. This general consensus was ingrained into
everyone's thinking. Here's a common opinion:

> The demonstration that no combination of known
> substances, known forms of machinery, and known
> forms of force can be united in a practicable machine
> by which men shall fly long distances through the air,
> seems to the writer as complete as it is possible for the
> demonstration of any physical fact to be. But let us dis-
> cover a substance a hundred times as strong as steel,
> and with that, some form of force hitherto unsuspected
> which will enable us to utilize this strength, or let us
> discover some way of reversing the law of gravitation
> so that matter may be repelled by the earth instead of
> attracted – then we may have a flying-machine. But we
> have every reason to believe that mere ingenious con-
> trivances of our present means and forms of force will

be as vain in the future as they have been in the past.

— *Dr. Simon Newcomb, Side-Lights on Astronomy,*
  1906

Dr. Newcomb was a famous scientist and mathematician of his day. He contributed many valuable theories and insights to science. Unfortunately, this wasn't one of them. As a matter of fact, notice the date of this quote: 1906. If you remember your history, you know that the Wright brothers demonstrated powered flight in December 1903 – three years earlier!

Why was Newcomb out of step? Wasn't he at the forefront of scientific research? Newcomb didn't acknowledge the Wright brothers' feat because he was very comfortable with the way things were. He was comfortable in the belief that this couldn't be done, so he didn't *expect* it to be done.

Actually, nearly the entire nation felt that way. What's more, for three years after their first flight, the Wrights continued test flights around a meadow near Dayton, Ohio. No one bothered them. No one noticed. A train track ran right along the edge of the field. Every day, passengers could look out the windows and see Orville or Wilbur flying around and around in this big box-kite contraption. Any day, some eager newspaper reporter could have scooped the world, but none did. Hence, the world remained almost entirely ignorant of the Wrights' wonderful discovery.

In addition to this incredible indifference, in some cases, the feat was even strenuously denied! Here's what a 1906 article in *Scientific American* said about the Wrights' rumored experiments:

> If such sensational and tremendously important experiments are being conducted in a not very remote

part of the country, on a subject in which almost everybody feels the most profound interest, is it possible to believe that the enterprising American reporter, who, it is well known, comes down the chimney when the door is locked in his face – even if he has to scale a fifteen-story sky-scraper to do so – would not have ascertained all about them and published them broadcast long ago?

In other words, the writer of the *Scientific American* article was opining that if you haven't read it in the paper, it hasn't happened. Well, the Wrights were hardly keeping their business a secret. Upon finishing that first successful flight at Kitty Hawk, they sent out press releases to several newspapers. A few newspapers picked up the story, such as this December 19, 1903, article from the Raleigh *Morning Post*:

Flying Machine Sustains Itself

Experiment at Kitty Hawk Pronounced a Success.

Good Speed in the Teeth of a Moderate Gale Up the Coast.

Norfolk VA December 19th — A successful trial of a flying machine was made yesterday at Kitty Hawk North Carolina by Wilbur and Orville Wright of Dayton OH. The machine flew three miles in the face of the wind blowing at a registered velocity of 21 miles an hour, then gracefully descended to the earth at the spot selected by the man in the navigator car as a suitable landing place. The machine has no balloon attachment, but gets its force from propellers worked by a small engine. During the trial Wilbur Wright occupied the operator's seat and guided the apparatus.

For three years the Wrights have experimented at Kitty Hawk with their invention. They chose that point because of its isolation and the absence of publicity. By the merest chance the success became known, as neither of the men is ready to make public the details of their machine.

The flight began from a platform constructed on a high sand hill near Kitty Hawk. There was no starting apparatus used to give momentum to the huge birdlike affair. When all was ready Wilbur Wright took his place in the car in the center of the machine and his brother released the catch which held the affair to the top of the incline. Gravity did the rest and while a rush down the slope was going on the navigator started a small gasoline engine in the floor of the car by a system of pulleys and cogs; this engine put into motion a six-bladed propeller directly beneath it [sic] and another extending horizontally to the rear. The first is used to maintain elevation and the other to propel the machine.

But instead of losing elevation when the end of the platform was reached, the machine continued its flight undisturbed, and as the under propeller increased its revolutions the machine gradually pointed upward and soon had attained the height of 60 feet above the rolling sand dunes.

A stiff wind was blowing up the Coast and the start was made directly into the teeth of it without difficulty and maintained an even speed of eight miles an hour with ease. The small crowd of fisher folk and life guards who had been curiously watching the construction of the machine for months, followed beneath it with exclamations of wonder and it soon drew away from them and went on its flight through the air alone. The first mile was covered, and then Orville Wright declared the invention was a success.

The Wrights have used a box kite idea in their invention and their flying machine is really an immense kite, with propellers and steering attachment. Its frame is of wood, stretched with canvas, and its dimensions as accurately as can be secured are here given: Width 33 feet from tip to tip; depth from front to rear five feet height also five feet. In the center of this frame is constructed the navigator car, while the engine below it serves as ballast. Directly beneath the car, and arranged to point upward, is the immense propeller used for elevating the machine, and extending horizontally to the rear is the propeller that gives the forward momentum [sic]. A rudder spread with canvas extended 13 feet forward and spread like a fishtail and kept the machine straight to the wind. The total area of the machine surfaces is exactly 206 square feet.

The Wrights knew they could fly, but no one believed it. This became frustratingly clear in an exchange of letters between the Wrights and the U.S. government. A little over a year after they first flew on December 17, 1903, Wilbur and Orville Wright sent a letter to their congressman: "The series of aeronautical experiments upon which we have been engaged for the past five years has ended in the production of a flying machine of a type fitted for practical use. It not only flies through the air at high speed, but it also lands without being wrecked."

The congressman turned the letter over to the War Department, which, after a time, replied. Here's part of the response from Major General G. L. Gillespie of the War Department's general staff: "...as many requests have been made for financial assistance in the development of designs for flying machines, the Board has found it necessary to decline... The device must have been brought to the stage of practical operation..."

The Wrights were disappointed with this response, as you might imagine. They actually had a working machine, but the brass in the War Department couldn't seem to grasp the fact that it actually worked. So Orville and Wilbur decided to make their plane's abilities very clear. They sent another letter to the War Department, this time with a very tempting offer: "Some months ago we made an offer to furnish to the War Department practical flying-machines. We are prepared to furnish a machine on contract, to be accepted only after trial trips, in which the machine (shall) carry an operator and fuel sufficient for a flight of 100 miles, minimum speed 25 miles per hour."

The response from the War Department? It recommended "that Messrs. Wright be informed that the Board does not care to formulate any requirements for the performance of a flying machine or to take any further action on the subject until a machine is produced which by actual operation is shown to be able to produce horizontal flight and to carry an operator."

That obviously canned response did it. The Wrights took their invention somewhere else. In this case, overseas. They made successful flights in France and Germany and began negotiations with both the French and German militaries for the purchase of flying machines. Once the "experts" in the U.S. War Department found out about the French and the German interest, they got busy and contacted the Wrights. In short order, they arranged for flight tests – in 1908.

But notice that 1908 was *five years* after the Wrights had first flown.

The moral of the story: Depending on what your invention is, "experts" can actually get in your way. They are generally blinded by their own stature. They see things from the great height of their own reputation, and that means they don't see things very clearly. They have turf to protect, they are biased, and this bias will keep them from really understanding what your idea is all about.

Businesspeople

You could take your terrific idea to someone you know in an unrelated field, who might be willing to give you an opinion of it from a business perspective. This might be valuable, but at best, the advice would be incomplete. If the businessperson isn't in a field that's close to your idea, he or she won't know the state of the art. The businessperson probably can tell you about business conditions, but not about how to make your idea into a product, how to sell it, who to sell it to – or if it's even worth the investment.

Well, you probably knew it was coming to this. But at the end of the day, the only person you can trust absolutely is *yourself.*

You can trust yourself to be truthful. You won't have another agenda. You will look out for your own interest, and you will do a thorough job of it. The only problem is, you don't know what questions to ask, and often you aren't going to like the answers you get.

CHAPTER 5

What You Must Be Willing to Do

Wouldn't it be nice if you could hire someone, so you could avoid the ordeal of taking your product out into the big, wide world? That's the siren call that every inventor hears. It seems to be so easy to let someone else do it, but more often than not, it won't work. The fact is that ideas are rarely sold by people who didn't develop them. Why?

Consider this: To convince a company to buy your idea, you have to present it to people who are in that business. They know a lot about their business because they work in it every day. At best, you are at a disadvantage because your information is older than theirs. You don't have access to their internal memoranda. You don't know what their sales figures are. You don't know a lot about the internal politics of their business. But at least you have an understanding of the business, because you've invented something that would be useful to them. You are the expert, as far as your idea is concerned.

Now, consider someone else. They might know more about the field, but do they really understand your invention? Do they have the same insight that you do? Probably not. And there is something much more important than that: Do you think they would have the same passion as you do? They assuredly do not.

Would you trust your baby to someone who actually didn't care very much about it? Someone who didn't know anything about it? Would you rely on a hired hand to sell it to people

who know all there is to know about their business? Don't
you imagine there will be some questions that will come up
that the marketing firm or lawyer you engage to pitch your
idea can't answer? They might be very smart, but have they
studied the market from your perspective? Will they know
why you designed the product to work the way it did? Will
they understand why you invented it in the first place?

That's why you must be there at the presentation. As a
matter of fact, you *want* them to ask you, "Why did you do
this? Why did you see it this way and not that way? Why didn't
you do this?"

You want to be there because you have the passion. You
have the interest. You can be counted upon either to fix any
problems or, once you are made aware of problems, to be able
to work with your client to solve them. You are going to be
motivated to do whatever it takes to get your invention over.

Would someone else? I doubt it. It's not their baby.

I realize that most inventors are self-conscious and un-
easy when it comes to pitching their ideas. It's something
new. It's going to make you uncomfortable. You are not a
public speaker. I know how you feel. Does it help to know
that everyone feels that way? Does it help for me to tell you
that the moment you open your mouth to talk about your
baby you won't be able to shut up? What parent doesn't like
to talk about their baby? But right now, before you are in the
meeting room, it seems like a pretty steep hill to climb, and
that makes you vulnerable. So, look out! That fear of the
unknown could set you up for a very painful and expensive
lesson.

Everyone knows how you feel, and some of the people
who know it are going to try to take advantage of you. They
know that most people with an idea are afraid and uncertain
about how to proceed. They know that a lot of inventors with

an idea are willing to pay someone else to do the difficult part of the job, just so they don't have to. They know that they can make a very fat living off the folks who just want to dream something up and then back away, leaving all the salesmanship and sweat to someone else. They are looking for someone who doesn't want to get his or her hands dirty. Don't be one of these inventors!

I'm sure you've seen ads on TV or received letters from marketing hypesters who promise you the moon. Why, if they were to be believed, you would think they have a secret list of customers all primed and ready to buy your wonderful widget. It's probably not true.

The fact remains that your idea is just one more idea in a large pile of ideas that come across their desk every day. The only reason they don't yawn when you talk to them is because they are afraid they won't get your money if they act as bored as they really are. This has nothing to do with how good your idea is. This has to do with their business. They need clients. The more the merrier. To them, your idea is piecework. They want to handle you and cash your check. It's just business.

Your idea is a specific part of you that is unique, and it demands a lot of study to completely grasp. You came up with the idea because you are the inventor. Do you seriously think that someone who doesn't know you and hasn't a clue how you came up with this idea will be able to represent you? Is it going to be worth it to pay her by the hour to go through the same learning curve you did, just so she can get up to speed – if it's even possible for her to get up to speed?

There is only one party you'll need to get up to speed: your customer. This is not to say that at some point you aren't going to need support. You will need a good lawyer. You will need a good advertising or marketing agency. But you must use them at the right time. And when you are getting the idea off the ground is definitely not the right time. They will be needed later.

A patent lawyer writes patents. A corporate lawyer writes contracts. That's it. You need them then. Lawyers are paid to read fine print and understand the law. They aren't salespeople.

Most marketing firms have no special expertise when it comes to representing your idea. Marketing firms are advertising agencies. They know media, they know public relations, and they know promotion. These are all skills that are going to be needed after you take your product to market.

You aren't ready for any of those things yet. You don't even have a product sold yet. Why would you advertise or promote something that doesn't yet exist?

When you approach a company's people with an idea, it is truly a David and Goliath confrontation. The company has all the experience, brainpower, and customers. You have your clever idea and a lot of pluck. It's not a fair match. They spend every working day trying to improve the product they sell. They test and analyze their product constantly. You would think that with all the testing and analyzing they would ultimately exhaust just about every variation possible, wouldn't you? So it should come as no surprise if most of the ideas that they see have already been gone over and rejected.

In short, there is a reason a company hasn't thought of your idea, and the most probable reason is that its people thought of it, all right, and then decided that it wasn't worth pursuing. If this happens to you, be careful and keep a cool head. Yes, it's disappointing. Ouch, it hurts. But don't go off the deep end just because someone says "not interested," and for goodness sake don't let your feelings run away with you. It can cost you a lot.

Many times, if the market for a newly invented product is too small for a big company, the inventor will decide to sell the product himself. He or she will think, "Who cares if the market is too small for this great big company with all these employees. I'll just sell it myself and make all the money. HA to them."

Now, this is sad, because when an inventor tries to sell his or her own invention, suddenly he or she is no longer an inventor anymore; he becomes something altogether different and probably someone he or she shouldn't be. Suddenly, the inventor turns into an entrepreneur, and that might not be the best thing to happen to you. Some people are naturals – they actually like running businesses and going it alone. But that might not be you.

Going into business to make your widget is a tall order, and for that reason, it is almost always a very bad idea when an inventor transforms from an inventor into a manufacturer. As clever as the inventor may be, he doesn't have the experience to also go into the business of selling his own invention. If you think you might like to go down that path, let me give you an idea of what you face.

A business needs a product to sell. That's no problem – you have this little widget. That means you have to have a production facility to make it. So you'll get some guy to whip up a batch in his garage. Then you will need a sales department to sell it. No problem; you can sell it door to door. Or better yet, put up a Web site and have people clicking away to get at this wonderful widget.

No. Wait a minute. How will people know about the Web site or the 800 number or the mailing address? OK, you will have to advertise.

Now, all this costs money, doesn't it? So let's say you give a few thousand to the guy who makes it, and put in some money for an advertising agency to design and place the ad, and then a little more to buy the media space and... well, you see why I say this can be a very bad idea.

Most inventors don't want to be manufacturers; they want to be inventors. Often (though not always) they aren't very good at promotion and marketing their product, and frankly, most don't have the kind of deep pockets that selling it themselves is going to require. You can spot a disappointed inventor-turned-entrepreneur easily. They don't have the moxy to sell their product properly and it shows.

That's why you see all those little two-inch ads in the back of magazines. The inventors of the clever gadgets advertised have decided to manufacture and market the gadgets themselves. I would imagine most of these little gizmos will do what they are advertised to do. But as you thumb through the magazine ads, ask yourself this question, How many customers are there for this particular idea?

Notice the question is not, *Are* there any customers? The question is, *How many?* Certainly, there are *some* customers, but are there enough to pay back the investment the inventor has to make to produce and sell the product?

Even if an inventor is wise enough to stay away from trying to sell it directly to the public, he or she still might get tripped up by another type of ad that also appears in some magazines. These are sharpies that target frustrated inventors who have been turned down by companies one too many times. This time, it's not an offer to pitch your idea to a potential customer; this time, it's a much bigger promise. Why, these folks are going to bring this brilliant-but-underappreciated widget to market by getting the invention patented, manufactured, advertised, and shipped without any effort from the inventor. They will do it all. All the inventor has to do is pay for it. This is equivalent to letting someone else do all the heavy lifting – the protection, the manufacturing, the advertising, the fulfillment, the works. They say they will do what a big company would do. But remember, there is a difference.

A big company sells a lot of items in this particular market, so their manufacturing, advertising, and fulfillment operations are busy 24-7. They do it every day. They have a built-in customer base. They have credibility and a track record. They're probably well known and respected, and most importantly, they have brand recognition that has been built up in this particular field over the years.

But our hapless and frustrated inventor has none of this. So what about the company that *says* it has all of these capabilities? Well, it would be mighty odd if this particular marketing company had a customer base that was specifically interested in this widget. Why would they? They aren't in that particular business, are they? They don't have any of the specific contacts that a manufacturer of items in that field would. And will they be as good at marketing, production, sales, distribution, and so forth as a company already in the field? No, they probably won't have any of those assets.

So, instead of a targeted market all primed to purchase, this general marketing company just has a general kind of market that is made up, probably, of some of the same folks that little ad would reach anyway. In short, their "eager and interested market" won't be very eager or very interested.

I'm not saying that this general-market company isn't going to sell any of these gizmos, but it takes a lot of gizmos to actually become a thriving business. And remember, the real market is probably not very large – that's why the big guy, who knows that particular market inside out, turned the idea down in the first place.

Considering all the obstacles and downright fraud that can trip up a would-be entrepreneur, one wonders why anyone would want to go this route.

There may be a lot of reasons, but it all comes down to emotion and hurt feelings. Remember, this idea is the inventor's baby. It hurts to get turned down time and again. So finally, after spending so much effort, it's very tempting to try to sell the item directly. Sometimes it hurts so much that nice people who really can't afford it go into the manufacturing business just to prove the other guy was wrong and to justify all the time they've spent on the invention.

We don't want you to spend your money and time on an idea that will end up costing you more money and time than it's worth. The best way to prevent that is to make sure that the product you have actually has a real market and that the market is large enough to support a large-scale effort. If it does, then you can rest assured that it will generate some large-scale interest from a large-scale company that has the wherewithal to put some real muscle behind that idea of yours.

See what I mean? Your idea is a unique one. It is a child of your mind, conceived to accomplish a specific task or solve a specific problem. Why would a marketing firm or a lawyer be able to represent you? There are no ropes they know that you don't know. All they may be able to do to benefit you is to help you prepare a slick presentation.

There is one exception to the rule that inventors should not become their own entrepreneur: If you are well acquainted with the field, you have an edge. But you must have an invention that springs directly from your day-to-day knowledge of the field, not one that just occurred to you one day. The difference between a true understanding of the field and a superficial one will spell the difference between success and failure.

Here's an example of someone who was a true expert and made the most of his idea: I have a good friend who had a good idea. He figured out a way to splice cable that would save time and manpower. He knew it was a good idea because he'd worked in the field for years. He had started at the lowest position in that field, and after a number of years he rose to middle management. He knew what a good idea he had because he had seen the need, up close and personal. He had developed the idea because he needed it and the people who worked for him needed it. He developed the idea because he was close to it. Fingertip close. Bruised-thumb close. He was an insider in this industry, not someone from the outside looking in.

So he went to his boss and presented his idea. He asked his boss to take it to his employer's management. He took it through all the proper channels. With all that going for him, you would have thought his job would be easy.

Hardly. Just like the government dealing with the Wright brothers, my friend's management had turf to protect. They had channels to follow. They weren't about to rock any boats. They had a successful business here and they weren't about to make any drastic changes.

They thought about it. They talked about it. Then one day, he got called into his boss's office and was told, "We've decided we don't want to use this idea."

Was my friend brokenhearted? Was he even disappointed? Nope! He was delighted! Why? Because he'd already made the most important decision of his life. Without batting an eye, he said, "Well, if you don't want it, can I have it?"

As he'd hoped, they said yes, and they signed all rights to

it over to him. My friend then made the second most fateful decision of his life: He left the company.

He started a little business that made his new splicing device. He took on the role of personally handling every task the company required. He made the product, sold it, showed customers how to use it. It was a really tenuous operation at the beginning. He knocked on a lot of prospects' doors. But potential customers were used to running cable the tried-and-true way. My friend got turned down again and again, but he never lost faith in his little idea.

Finally, realizing the market in the United States was closed, he took his idea overseas. He knew this business and it showed. He banged on desks, he gave demonstrations, he climbed up poles. He did whatever it took to get his customers to see how important this idea was. Finally, after all that, he managed to sell some splicers. Then he sold a few more, and then a few more. After a lot of sacrifice, he came back to the States with a going concern.

More and more people started using his device. After a while, his splicers became widespread. Finally, his phone rang one day and it was an executive from his old company calling. I wish I had been there to hear it.

The exec said, "Say, that's a pretty good little company you have there. We want to buy it from you."

And they did. My friend got a pile of money for his business and retired. They bought his entire company, lock, stock, and barrel.

So, if you want to go into business making your widget or whatever, you must be like my friend who invented the cable splicer. You must believe. But I'm not talking about faith. I'm talking about a belief based on experience and knowledge. You must believe because you have the experience to *know* that you have a good idea. Not just a wish. You have to know, positively, because you have experience in the field.

There's something else that you can learn from my friend, whether you are going to sell this yourself or sell it to someone else. You must be willing to keep at it – and this does require faith. This time it's faith in yourself and your own good judgment. This is not the same thing as hope that you're doing the right thing. Any dope can hope. You are going to need more than hope to get you over the rough spots. Doors will be slammed in your face, but you must keep going forward. It can get pretty tiring, having doors slammed in your face, and only faith will get you through. But in the final analysis, it is this faith – this passion – that will enable you to make the sale.

That belief in your idea is contagious. It's infectious. It's critical to your success. For a company to want to invest in a new idea, they need something besides your idea, something which only you can provide to them. Only you can give them commitment. Only you can provide the vision and the fire in the belly that any good CEO wants to see.

A good CEO knows that as you work your idea into his or her company, there will be some bruised feelings and some problems. There are always problems – they come with the territory. CEOs want somebody pushing the idea to make sure it happens. That somebody should be you.

I remember sitting in a boardroom with the senior vice president of marketing of a very large company. I must admit, the surroundings really were impressive. This was the executive conference room where the board of directors met. This was the place where multibillion-dollar acquisitions were made. The walls were paneled in rich mahogany. There was a long conference table with pads of paper, jugs of water, bottles of juice, and snacks at every seat. The room had absolutely state-of-the-art equipment for videoconferencing and presentations. There was gorgeous artwork on the walls. The setting was imposing.

I was there with the upper management of the company. I was presenting an idea that was going to be difficult to sell because it required that several of their brands combine. This is like trying to put several lions in the same cage. Brand managers have separate budgets and jealously protect their allocations, and I was forcing them to pool their resources. This was going to be difficult and I knew it. So did the senior VP of marketing, and that's why he was there. He was the only guy senior enough to crack the whip and make these lions behave. As a matter of fact, that is why we met in the board of directors' conference room. He wanted to impress his own people. They had never been up to the top floor, either. The surroundings said that this meeting was important.

The senior VP began the meeting and introduced the company's managers. Then he introduced me, and what he said in introducing me underscores why you must be at the presentation meeting for your own idea.

He said, "Gentlemen, I want you to meet Mr. Kamille. He is the inventor of this. He has personally sold every one of you on this program. He has sold me on this program, as well. He has put everything he has into this program. And that's why I know it will be a success."

Do you get it? The senior VP was looking for commitment, because he knew that nothing happens without it. Only you, the originator of your idea, have that kind of commitment, because it's your idea. Commitment is a product of certainty.

In business, most of what we do is just routine. To break into the clear requires something beyond the regular day-today effort. It requires a drive to excel. Some people have lots of it, some have very little. A good CEO looks for that type of drive in staff members. They are the team. They carry the ball. You – as an inventor bringing an idea to the company – are applying to be on the team. You have to show the CEO and subordinates how committed you are.

That commitment means you will do whatever it takes to get your idea across. You can show your commitment in lots of little ways that really impress people, because they don't expect it.

For instance, I live on the West Coast and wanted to get a meeting with a company headquartered on the East Coast. I kept calling the senior VP of marketing, trying to set up a meeting, but I never could get through. I was just one call out of lots of calls. So I finally decided to take an extra step to get his attention.

This potential customer happened to be a very large supermarket chain. I had a packaged-goods product I wanted the senior VP to see. I know that supermarket people start work early in the day – it's not unusual for them to get into the office by 7 a.m. They have to get the trucks out of the warehouses and on the road early to get to the stores before the shoppers empty those shelves. So I rose at 4 a.m. (heeding the three-hour time zone difference) and made the call. It went like this:

He (sleepily): "Hello."

Me: "Mr. – – , I'm calling you from L.A., and it's four in the morning here. I got up a little early because I want to talk with you before your phones start ringing, and I felt this was the best way."

His reaction? Well, first he laughed.

He: "Are you always such an early bird?"

Me: "No, but I've got lots of calls to make and you are at the top of the list. I want you to have first shot at this product before I sell it to your competition. And Mr. – – , you know I'll sell it, don't you?"

He: "Yes, I imagine you sure as hell will."

Then we both laughed.

And I got my product on the shelf.

What happened here? I gave him what any good CEO wants: commitment. Clients want to see that you will get up early and push to make something happen. It's unusual to see. Most employees just take their paycheck and try to figure a way to get through the day. When someone comes at a CEO with flames shooting out his or her exhaust pipe, it's impressive. CEOs don't see that every day.

That fire-in-the-belly phenomenon has got to be you. That's what it's going to take to sell your idea – enthusiasm and passion. Not at every juncture of the negotiations, of course. But at just the right time you must show the customer that you are uncommonly committed and will stick to it. I'd want that kind of person on my team, wouldn't you?

Commitment is easy to generate when it's your idea. It is naturally generated by your idea. Your idea is a child of your mind. It's you. If it's good, it's the best part of you. So don't worry if you aren't the best presenter in the world. Don't worry if you have difficulty selling. When you are in that room with all these people waiting for you to describe your baby, it's easy. You're talking about your baby, and you know every dimple and curl. This isn't something you're unsure of. You put this together. You've thought it through. So you're going to be confident. You're going to be sure of yourself.

That's what your customer wants to see.

CHAPTER 6

What Does This Idea Have?

Has it ever occurred to you that you might not have an invention in the first place? You might *think* you have an invention. It might *seem* to be an invention. But is it?

Obviously, you can't very well go to a company with a widget you've invented tucked under your arm, only to find out that not only isn't it an invention but also your prospective client rejected the basic idea long ago. Yet it happens all the time.

The reason would-be inventors have difficulty telling whether their invention is really an invention is because they confuse "invention" with "marketing." Marketing is a means of presenting a product in a certain light to make it desirable to a certain group of potential purchasers. An invention is a novel device that is produced to appeal to a certain group of potential purchasers who might never have known they wanted something like that before.

For example, Post-its are truly an invention. The idea of making a product out of a little piece of paper that didn't actually stick very well is really novel. On the other hand, purple, red, and green Post-its are marketing variations of the original idea. Colored Post-its are attempts to increase the sales of the original Post-it product. Color-coding the product gives the consumer more ways to use it. That means the consumer will buy more of the same basic product for a slightly enhanced use. The different colors don't make the product novel; they make it more appealing. That's marketing not inventing. Most companies offer a lot of marketing in place of novel products. Often, *they* don't know the difference, either.

You, the inventor, might fall victim to the same confusion. Take a look at that idea of yours and consider whether it is an enhancement of or a variation on an already existing product. If it is and you plan to take it to the manufacturer and get them to pay you for it, look out! Chances are you actually might not have anything to sell.

Directors of new product development tell me that this is the most common "invention" companies see. Dozens of times a day, they get calls for appointments from sincere people who have nothing but a good twist on a product that already exists. And most often, the company already thought about the variation or enhancement and turned it down!

There are a lot of reasons the company may have turned the product down, but the most common reason is that the market just isn't there. It could be that the variation is too expensive to make or too difficult to distribute. Remember the rules we mentioned in Chapter 3: market sensitivity, return on investment, cannibalism, and impact on the industry? If the idea violates one of the cardinal rules, no one will touch it. Whatever the reasons, if a company has already thought of it and discarded the idea, then why should they pay you for it?

In evaluating your idea, you have to realize that the person who is going to make the most trouble for you is the person you see in the mirror every morning when you brush your teeth. You are going to be your own worst enemy in this process. Why? Because you thought it up – and now you have to figure out why your terrific idea is not so terrific.

To ensure your idea is doable, you have to be your own

devil's advocate. This is difficult because you already have invested a lot of hopes and emotions in this idea of yours and you don't want to let go of the hope.

I understand. I've been in just those shoes. Over the years, however, I've learned that you must be dispassionate when analyzing your idea, because everyone else is going to be. Real experts are going to look at your wonderful idea as if it were an exotic bug. They are going to scrutinize it with a magnifying glass and try to detect something wrong with it. If they do discover a flaw, they will be able to brush you off and get on with the really important things in their lives – such as lowering their golf scores or running their businesses. You will have been just an interruption in their busy day.

If you want your idea to be successful, you need to consider its originality, its manufacturability, its salability, and its similarity to other, comparable products. To help you decide where your product fits, I advise you to use a checklist of questions like the one on the next page. It's a way to give your wonderful widget that cold, hard look we were talking about. This is where it gets difficult. Yes, I know it's your baby, but Baby needs a thorough checkup to make sure it will grow up and reach its full potential.

A serious analysis means you must answer every question truthfully. Then you must count up the yeses and nos. There is no correct number of yeses and nos. The purpose here is to get a picture of your idea from the point of view of the different people who will ultimately have to pass judgment on its salability.

It's a walk around the idea to put it in a different perspective. Certainly, it looks good from your point of view. You thought it up. But how will it look to people who have never seen a new item like the one you have designed? They are going to ask you lots of questions, and you must have good answers.

CONCEPT EVALUATION

	DEFINITELY +4	MODERATELY +2	AVERAGE +1	NO −1
ORIGINALITY				
1. Improvement in field				
2. Unique in field				
3. Adds something different				
4. Would competition want it?				
5. Would you pay for it?				
SUBTOTAL				
MANUFACTURABILITY				
6. Simple to make				
7. Ready to go now				
8. Made by present equipment				
9. Familiar manufacturing method				
10. Cheap to make				
11. Easy to use				
12. Easy to understand				
13. Maintenance free				
14. Require unskilled labor				
15. Easily available materials				
SUBTOTAL				
SALABILITY				
16. Profitable in small amounts				
17. Easy to get distribution				
18. Already a section in a store				
19. Easy to get space on shelf				
20. Easy to explain to a buyer				
21. Easy for customer to understand				
22. Ready, willing, and able market				
23. Easy to get sales force support				
SUBTOTAL				
FAMILIARITY				
24. Similar to something well known				
25. Short learning curve				
26. Easy to use				
27. Efficient to use				
28. Obvious benefit				
SUBTOTAL				

	Originality	Manufacturability	Salability	Familiarity
TOTALS				
GRAND TOTAL		Your product's overall score divided by 28		

Compare your overall score with the scores below
to give you an idea of the appeal of your product.

Highest Possible	112
Moderate	56
Average	28
Poor	−28

Keep in mind that if you don't have the answers to these questions now, you shouldn't despair. You can always fix that. But consider the consequences if you don't have the answers while you're in a meeting with a judge and jury ready to pounce upon a simple, overlooked item! You'll be sunk. So be hard on your idea. This will greatly increase its value when it comes time to talk money.

Finally, don't assume that your idea has to be a widget – not all highly profitable inventions are physical things. Often, they are processes or methods for reducing costs by reducing labor, the amount of materials needed, the weight of a manufactured item, and so forth. If you have a system that can produce someone else's product more cheaply or at a better quality or more quickly, then you have something of value. There is a market for that value and you can make real money from that market. Sometimes you don't even need to sell the process; you can just lease the equipment and collect additional revenue based on the number of parts run across the system. Your great idea might end up being something unique that no one else could provide but that can be applied to someone else's product to improve their efficiency.

Whether it is a widget or a process, thinking about it from all these different angles will help you get a fresh view on what you really have. So let's look at each of these in order: its originality, its manufacturability, its salability, and its resemblance to other products – its familiarity.

Originality

How do you determine originality?

First, ask yourself whether this is something that you have seen before. Is it an improvement of something that is currently being sold? Does it do something differently than other kinds of products in the same field? Will it improve a company's profits or expand the market? Does your idea do something a similar product cannot do? Does it do something so much better than your potential customer's current product that your customer's competition would want it? If you saw it on a shelf, would you say, "Gee, isn't that a good idea. Why hasn't anyone thought of that before?" If the reason no one has thought of it before is because it couldn't be done before, then it's probably original. And while you're standing in front of that shelf, ask yourself this question: How much is it worth to me to own it?

Value depends on what an idea does and how much people will pay for what it does. The operative words here are *how much*. Will people pay a dollar for a really good cup of coffee? Yes, it would appear they will. Will they pay two dollars? Well, Starbucks doesn't seem to have much trouble getting it. How about three dollars? Now the terrain gets a little steeper, doesn't it? I suppose if the cup of coffee were a bit *more* than just a cup of coffee, people would pay three dollars. But at some point the desire will not be strong enough to support the cost – the point just below that is the value of an item.

Value depends upon the size of the market and the cost of bringing that item to market. If there's a large market and low cost to get it to market, someone can make some substantial money from it. That makes the idea valuable. If there's a small market but the item can command a very large price, then it still might be valuable. The more value an item has, the easier it will be to get a company to want to own it. If it's something the market has been looking for with bated breath, you've got yourself a hot item. If there are several products that do the same thing and your idea isn't that different, there's not much value, and that means there will not be much interest.

One key element can help you determine the value of your invention: Can the ownership of the rights to make your invention hurt the competition? If it can change the leadership of a company in a particular market, then you will have an easy time selling it. Everyone in the field will be bidding for it. There's an old real estate saying that applies to inventions too: "One offer is just an offer. Two offers make a sale." The minute you have more than one customer interested, you have competition; this means your price goes up and your invention can easily be sold.

Manufacturability

Just how simple is this to make? Will it work without a lot of additional input from someone else? Will the idea work without further engineering or does it require someone else to do a lot to make it actually operate? Remember, the more someone else puts into this idea, the more they have invested in it – and, therefore, the less you can take out of it.

A good way to gauge this is to ask yourself whether present equipment can make it or you need to have an entirely new manufacturing method. Needless to say, new manufacturing methods are not a plus if any potential client is going to have to come up with it on their nickel.

How is it made? Can it be made and distributed cheaply? Once it's made, is it easy to understand how it's used? Can a salesperson describe it to a customer without a complicated manual? Is it rugged enough to be used frequently without a lot of adjustments or breakdowns? Frankly, complicated and

delicate inventions are difficult to sell and very hard to
make money on. If you or your client have to keep fixing it,
that cost gets subtracted from your profit. So, if it's fragile,
forget it. You'll spend all your profits keeping it operating.

Just how difficult is this going to be to put into a box? Is it
going to be simple to assemble? Is it going to be easy and
quick to make? Can untrained people make it or does it require highly skilled labor? The easier and less demanding it
is to make, the more a manufacturer can make on it. The
more they can make on it, the easier it will be for you to sell
it to them.

Salability

Your idea must be sold to be of value. Can it be sold in small
quantities at a profit? Is it going to be easy to get onto a shelf?
Is there already a section in a store where it would be
stocked? If not, what would have to come off that shelf to
make room for this product? Getting shelf space for a new
product is extremely difficult and expensive. The product
would have to have some very terrific potential to entice sell-
ers to make a hole on the shelf big enough to warrant stocking it. Can it be explained by a salesperson? Will consumers
understand how to use it immediately?

A negative answer to any of these questions is really going
to present you with a problem. Your customer is going to
want a ready, willing, and able market. If consumers need to
be educated before they can use it, then you are in big trouble. The general public is more conservative and less flexible
than the people you are trying to sell your idea to. That's because they can afford to be completely passive. Your customer
has to woo the public, and that means the sale is no longer in

your hands. Just how difficult will it be to get your potential customer's sales force to get the product on the shelf? How difficult will it be to motivate them?

I've spent the largest part of my business career motivating salespeople to sell product. Salespeople are your most important link in this long chain from production to shelf. If you can get them aboard, your idea will at least make it to the shelf. Then you get to the final and most important step: Will customers take it off the shelf and buy it?

Familiarity

Familiarity can be a big help in getting customers to take a product off the shelf and buy it. So just how similar is this new product to something that is well known? To be accepted, the general public has to understand what the product is and they have to easily "get it." A steep learning curve is the kiss of death. When television was introduced, it caught on quickly (once the programming was available of course). That's because it was similar to a radio, which consumers already understood. Early TV had two knobs – one to turn it on and off, and one to tune to various channels – just like radio. So consumers could say to themselves, "This is just a radio with pictures."

On the other hand, desktop computers didn't catch on instantly. Because computers use a TV monitor, you might think that the TV screen would make it seem familiar. In fact, that is what made it so hard. People saw the TV screen and thought the computer was a TV. But it doesn't work like a TV. It has no channels to change or volume to control. It uses a typewriter keyboard but it doesn't work like a typewriter. It's not a calculator but it has buttons like a calculator.

And then there's this "mouse," which everyone knows has nothing to do with making a typewriter or a calculator work but for some reason makes a computer work. Considering how different a computer is from anything most people had ever used, it's not surprising these new machines were held in air-conditioned clean rooms for so long.

Another big sticking point was that computers were very difficult to use. A company needed platoons of specialists just to keep them running. Over time, however, the computer was simplified and made much more user friendly, and as that occurred, more of them came into common use.

Computers are now so widespread that the idea of a typewriter that just types one sheet in the same font and with no formatting seems quaint and old-fashioned. But it took thirty years for that to happen. There's an important lesson here. Are you prepared to wait thirty years for your product to catch on? If you don't want to wait that long, keep your product familiar enough that consumers will easily understand how to use it.

PART II

Protecting Your Idea

CHAPTER 7

Establishing a Paper Trail

O K. You've analyzed and scrutinized your idea from every imaginable angle, ferreting out flaws. You've carefully considered the market for the product originating from your idea. You have a horseback guess as to how much it would cost to produce it and who would likely buy it. You can honestly say to yourself that at all times you were pre-pared to scrap your idea if it failed any of your tests – but it didn't. You played around with it, tweaked it, refined it over and over, and finally decided it was worth your precious time, effort, and savings to push ahead with. Now you're ready to take your terrific idea out into the big, wide world and present it to someone.

But there are a few things you need to do to protect that idea before you start showing it off. The idea at this stage is like a youngster. It needs to be protected. It can't protect it-self – you have to protect it. Earlier, we discussed the U.S. Patent and Trademark Office. The PTO requires that you be able to show that you are the unique inventor of your idea and came up with the idea out of your inventiveness, not be-cause you saw it on television or read about something simi-lar in a magazine. (The PTO does allow you to file for a patent if the idea has been available to the general public for less than a year, but only if you can show you came up with the idea first.)

So how do you show anyone – let alone the PTO – that you actually thought this widget up? You must write the idea down on a single piece of paper. Writing it down starts what is called a "paper trail," a series of baby steps committed to paper that show the development of your idea from the very first cocktail napkin you scratched the idea down on to the final, full-blown blueprint that will be used to actually create the product. Every time you refine the idea, write down what you thought. Write it down even if you later decide it isn't the way you want the idea to work. Writing it down shows you are working with it, thinking it through. By the way, keep all these little pieces of paper and – need I say it? – keep them safe.

Why try to write down your initial idea on just a single sheet? To focus your idea and help you summarize its benefits in a succinct manner. This will pay big dividends when you are talking to other people about your idea. It will keep you from rambling on and on about how great your idea is and making things up on the fly. If you can put your idea on a single sheet and in a summary form, it means you can get your fingers mentally around it, and as we'll discuss later, it is an important first step in gaining protection for your idea.

An idea has great promise, and the better the idea the greater the promise. However, what may seem clear to you might not be clear to someone else. That's why a succinct description that sums up the idea is so important. If your idea is really good, you can bet your bottom dollar that at some point you will have to prove to someone that it was your idea in the first place.

In Edison's day, inventors used a notebook. Every day, Edison wrote down what work on inventions he had done that day. He then signed it and had it witnessed. Those notebooks were often used in patent litigation cases involving his inventions. Writing his progress down each day also helped him remember what he had done previously and prevented him from duplicating work.

As I mentioned before, it isn't important if your first idea gets changed. Inventions are that way. The early work is the basis for the later, and courts understand that. A paper trail of cocktail napkins and scraps of paper is certainly better than just saying, "Hey, wait! I had that idea in 1996!"

The important thing to remember is that the court will look for evidence of sustained and serious work on the idea. The invention doesn't have to be in its final form. The work you've done doesn't even have to have led to the actual invention. Many times I have started out thinking I was inventing one thing, and before I knew it, found myself somewhere else, inventing something totally different. I just followed where the trail led me. The court will want evidence that you were working on it. A judge will want to see evidence of a paper trail.

So make this an ironclad rule: Put it on paper! The minute you have the idea, scratch it down on a piece of paper and date and sign it, even if it's on a cocktail napkin while sitting in a restaurant or bar. If you have a friend with you at the time, then get it witnessed. That means have your friend sign and date the napkin, too.

How strong is such protection? It depends. Most problems associated with ownership of an idea involve the date and time of invention. Alexander Graham Bell spent much of his time fighting lawsuits based on the hour that he filed for his telephone patent at the patent office. It nearly ruined his life. Can you imagine fighting lawsuits and arguing over your invention for years? It can happen.

But it's not as likely to happen if you sign and date everything. You can then form a chain of discovery. You can trace the development of your idea from its earliest glimmering to its final form. Notebooks, faxes, e-mails, and witnesses – verifying and chronicling the work you've done on your invention – are the lowest level of legal protection for your idea, and they are very important.

But let's move up a notch. Let's say that, at long last, you have your idea finished and you want to show it to a potential customer. You even have the perfect company in mind. Do you patent your idea? Do you apply for a copyright? Do you keep it secret? What do you do with it?

I can tell you one thing right off: Don't immediately run to your nearest patent attorney and start writing checks. There are several things you should do before spending money on lawyers and patents. These steps get increasingly complicated as you get closer to a deal and royalties, and they include the invention disclosure form and the nondisclosure agreement. Don't worry – samples of each are included in this chapter, so you don't have to call your lawyer yet.

Your invention disclosure form, or IDF, is basically that single sheet of paper you used to write down the idea. It will enable you to establish yourself as the inventor of that idea and to establish the time when you conceived of the idea.

In addition, you want to start showing that you are taking this idea seriously and are protecting it. How do you do that? You need to establish that a witness saw your idea, and most importantly, have him or her testify that they understood what they saw.

By the way, you are not doing this because you don't trust the person you're showing your idea to. I don't think your Uncle Charlie would steal your idea (at least, I hope not). In fact, anyone who signs an IDF is actually doing you a favor. The signer is helping you to continue that paper trail. If the person signs and dates the paper, he or she is witness to the fact that you had the idea in that form on that date. A written document that is signed and witnessed is a pretty solid piece of evidence that, on such and such a date, so-and-so actually saw this idea laid out.

On the next page, I've included the form that I use. You can design your own. There is nothing magical about the way mine is put together. The important thing is to include the word *confidential* on the header of the document so that it appears on every page. Then, all you have to do is have anyone who reads it sign and date it at the bottom.

Remember to keep the paper in a safe place. Easy, isn't it?

Now you have made a solid start in creating your paper trail. You have evidence that you are the inventor, and evidence of a date on which you showed your idea to someone. You have a witness to that fact. You also have a witness's agreement that they understood it and that they agree to keep it confidential.

I recommend you get at least two witnesses. I send one copy of my IDF to my accountant and one to my patent attorney. They are in different parts of the country. Because it would be nice to have something stronger than just a sworn statement from people I employ, I have my accountant take the copy across the hall to an attorney who works there and have him read it and sign it. I have never met that very helpful person. On the other end of the country, my patent attorney has his assistant sign it.

Are these two signed copies of the IDF incontrovertible evidence that the idea is truly mine? No. Should a dispute over ownership of the idea ever come to court, it certainly is possible to argue that all these people who saw and signed my IDF were lying on my behalf. They could all be secretly in my pay and will do anything I ask. But is it likely? No.

The next document you will need to have is a nondisclosure agreement, or NDA. It's just an agreement between you

CONFIDENTIAL
INVENTION DISCLOSURE FORM

Stuart J. Kamille, [DATE]
Invention Disclosure

This is to disclose a concept, which may result in an application for letters patent. Please review the material below and sign and date the document. Please indicate that you have read and understood the document by placing your initials next to the words,
"I have read and understood this disclosure."

[Put your description here]

SUBMITTED: Stuart J. Kamille, Page X of Y pages
DATE

[Now here's the part your witness signs.]

I have read and understood this disclosure and agree to keep the material herein described in confidence. _____
(PLEASE INITIAL)

SIGNATURE
DATE

and whomever you are going to show your idea to, indicating that they will keep confidential what you are describing.

Like IDFs, NDAs are generally very simple and serve to establish that your idea was shared only under the umbrella of a confidential relationship. It serves as evidence that the disclosure you have made was not meant to be made public. NDAs typically are used later in the process, when you are ready to present the idea to a customer.

The easiest way to protect your idea is to get your potential customer to say that he or she wants to see your idea and agrees not to use the idea without paying you for it. That would be nice (and cheap, too) – a very gentlemanly verbal agreement. The courts would probably recognize it. Unfortunately, we don't live in such gracious times, so you won't be able to get a company to agree to a verbal agreement.

The next easiest way is to get your potential customer to say in writing that the customer wants to see your idea and agrees not to use the idea without paying you for it. Then you keep a copy and the customer keeps a copy. That way, you're protected from the customer stealing your idea and the customer is protected from you claiming that he or she agreed to buy your idea. It makes the meeting very clean. The company can say, "Yes, we looked at the idea as described in this document. We didn't like it. We told Mr. X so. He left, and that's it." Mr. X can't claim that he showed the company more than he did; the company can't claim that it never heard of Mr. X's (or your) idea before.

You see, in these litigious times when there is a lawyer available to sue for damages for practically anything, companies have gotten very cautious. Who can blame them? There are a lot of sharp-eyed attorneys who are looking to get deep-pocketed companies to pay for all kinds of imagined damages.

Companies want to limit their exposure by sharply boxing in what you did and did not show them. They want to be able to prove that your revelation only went so far. That's why they like a document that is mutually signed and that strictly limits what you can show and what they can see.

On the next page is a sample of an NDA, which I invite you to use. There are different types of NDAs (you can find them online), and the type you use depends on your circumstances.

NDAs like the one I've shown you are used every day. I always use them. I have never shown an unpatented idea to anyone without having an NDA signed. Why?

Believe it or not, if you don't try to protect your idea, you can lose all the rights that you might have. You must demonstrate that you tried to keep the idea in confidence and tried to keep it from being exposed to the general public. This NDA is evidence of that nature, so it is important.

The beautiful thing about an NDA is that it costs very little. You don't even need an attorney to draft it – that is, if the company to which you're intending to show your idea accepts your NDA. Often, a company will have its own legal department. The lawyers in these departments love to draw up NDAs. If it's a big company, the NDA it will want from you should be pretty close to what I have shown you here, but the company's lawyers probably will give you a form they want you to use. That's OK – usually.

It's not OK if the company's NDA form has lots of other clauses, especially ones that mention rights or claims or ownership of patents. If the NDA you receive from any company strays pretty far from the sample I provided above, run, do not walk, to the best available attorney before you do anything more with this company.

NONDISCLOSURE AGREEMENT

This CONFIDENTIALITY AND NONDISCLOSURE AGREEMENT ("Agreement") is made and entered into as of _____, 20___ ("Effective Date") by and between _____ ("Discloser") and _____ ("Recipient"). The Recipient has requested certain information from Discloser in connection with consideration of a possible business transaction or relationship between Recipient and Discloser. In the course of their communications, each party may disclose certain information considered by that party to be confidential ("Confidential Information"). The party disclosing any Confidential Information ("Discloser") must mark it as "Confidential." Any verbal disclosures of Confidential Information will be designated as confidential at the time of the disclosure by the disclosing party ("Discloser"). The Recipient of Confidential Information agrees to maintain the confidence of Discloser's Confidential Information and to prevent its unauthorized dissemination and use; provided, however, that this Agreement shall impose no obligation on Recipient with respect to maintaining the confidence of Confidential Information that

1) is not disclosed in writing as "Confidential" as set forth above,

2) is generally known or available by publication, commercial use, or otherwise through no fault of Recipient,

3) is known by Recipient at the time of disclosure and is not subject to restriction,

4) is independently developed or learned by Recipient,

5) is lawfully obtained from a third party who has the right to make such disclosure, or

continues on the next page ⌐

6) is released for publication by Discloser in writing.

Recipient agrees not to use the Confidential Information for purposes other than those necessary to directly further the negotiations between the parties. Further, Recipient expressly agrees not to use the Confidential Information for its own account or for the account of a third party unless expressly authorized by Discloser in writing.

All Confidential Information remains the property of Discloser and no license or other rights in the Confidential Information is granted hereby. Recipient agrees to return all Confidential Information, including but not limited to all documentation, notes, plans, drawings, and copies thereof, to Discloser upon Discloser's written request.

Neither party has an obligation under this Agreement to purchase any service from the other party. Neither party has an obligation under this Agreement to offer for sale any service that is the subject of, or that incorporates, any Confidential Information. Recipient's duty to protect Discloser's Confidential Information expires _____ years from the date of this Agreement.

This Agreement may only be modified in writing signed by both parties.

This Agreement shall be governed by and construed in accordance with the laws of the State of [Your State].

This Agreement may be executed in counterparts.

[Customer Company]
Date: _____, 20XX   By:
                                 Title:

[You]
Date: _____, 20XX   By:
                                 Title:

Frequently, companies really don't want ideas from the outside because over the years it has become too big a hassle. Flaky inventors are constantly suing, claiming this company or that stole their idea. Companies figure that if they make it really hard to get in the door, most of the flakes will dissolve before they manage to get into the conference room. Companies make it hard to get a foot in their door by requiring you, the inventor, to give them all sorts of rights, to swear never to sue them, and things of that nature.

Sometimes it's OK to sign such a document, particularly if you know the people and trust them. Often it's just a matter of using your best judgment. If you really need to get in the door and there is absolutely no other way, you might have to sign an NDA that you don't really like. Of course, you can see whether the company will lighten up its requirements, but if they dig in, you will ultimately sign. I've done that several times and I've never regretted it. That doesn't mean it will always be OK. It means that I've been lucky.

For example, I once had to meet with a potential client about a product I had that I knew would be super. The company, on the other hand, had a policy that required, with no exceptions, that I sign over all rights before I met with its people. I certainly wasn't going to do that! So it was an impasse. They wanted to see what I had, and I wanted to show them, but they couldn't get around their own internal legal requirements, and they weren't going to change them just for me. So what to do?

I resolved the problem this way: I wrote a letter saying I wanted to show them a speculative idea (and establishing the date I first contacted them). I described the presentation document but didn't put anything about the idea in the letter. They, in turn, sent me a letter inviting me to a meeting to discuss the document I wanted to present, and agreed not to use anything contained in it. I answered, accepting the appointment and acknowledging that the only thing we were going to discuss was that specific document.

We had the meeting, and I showed them the idea, and I didn't have to sign the NDA they had prepared, nor did they. The letters, which served as a substitute, so restricted the possible claims I could make that they felt comfortable. Because I could only talk about what was in the document, and because they had that document right in front of them, they were comfortable that I couldn't claim anything outside of the document. I was happy because I had evidence that they had received the information from me and couldn't deny it.

Silly, wasn't it? But sometimes you have to do what it takes to get the job done. This was just a hiccup. They had a policy, and I had to respect that. I considered myself lucky that they would talk to me at all. By the way, they wouldn't have met with me, ordinarily. I knew some of the people, and they knew me. So they knew I was a serious guy with a serious product. That really is all an NDA is about, anyway. It shows you're serious. The NDA is the best way to go, if you can go that way.

CHAPTER 8

Five Ways to Protect Your Idea

I would be remiss if I didn't warn you about the next few chapters. They deal with protection and patent law. I am not a patent lawyer. I'm not a lawyer at all. Frankly, I couldn't be a lawyer even if I wanted to be. So, although I will try to give you my understanding of protection and patent law (and I suppose it isn't too bad), it may not be the way a lawyer would explain it to you. But if a lawyer was writing this, you would probably be asleep in just a few minutes. The subject matter can be deadly dull, and only a lawyer would enjoy reading it.

Nonetheless, that doesn't mean that you shouldn't read about this. You need to know how to protect your idea. It's your obligation to understand what rights you have and what a patent is and what claims are. And that's what's coming up next. So pour yourself several cups of coffee and give it a try. Here we go... the next step beyond the NDA.

Have you ever heard that old send-yourself-a-letter-through-the-mail bromide? I hear it on a regular basis whenever anyone wants to know about patent protection. Yes, you can write your idea down and mail it to yourself so you can obtain a postmark on the envelope. Then, so the story goes, because the envelope is sealed, you can prove to a court that you had the idea on such and such a date – you have a U.S. postmark to prove it.

Now, what could be wrong with that? Who wouldn't believe in the veracity of the U.S. Post Office? And the beautiful part is that it's cheap! No lawyers, no patent papers, no waiting. Why, it's positively masterful!

All it will cost you is the price of the stamp and... your idea! That's right. You can lose your idea to someone else. Think about it: Ten seconds with a teakettle and some hot water will steam open just about any envelope. Would you trust establishing the date you had your million-dollar idea to something that simple to counterfeit? Of course not. The courts won't, either. So don't take chances with your future. Learn what you need. Take it seriously. That means no shortcuts. You really have to know what legal protections are available to you. Do you?

Do you know whether you need a patent or a copyright? What about keeping your idea as a trade secret? What exactly is a patent, anyway? How long does it stay in force? What does it cost? When do you call in a patent attorney?

Patents cost money and take time. It's up to you to know what your rights are and what means you have to make sure you get paid for your effort. So how do you do that? Wouldn't it be great if you had all those answers all together in one little pile?

The good news is that patents, copyrights, and trademarks aren't difficult to secure. *Writing* patents is difficult. For that, you will probably need a patent attorney. But before you put your hard-earned money down, you will need to know what is patentable and what is not.

Another one of those fantasy daydreams that goes along with the business of selling ideas is the notion that if you have somehow gotten a patent, it means your idea is worth something. Well, here's a dirty little secret that no patent attorney will ever tell you: It's easy to get a patent. As a matter of fact, I absolutely guarantee that you can get a patent. That's why there are so many companies constantly advertising that they will get you a patent even if your idea is only half baked. Unfortunately, lots of people spend lots of money getting their ideas patented and then find out that no one wants to buy them. Please don't let that be you.

Getting a patent is a snap. That's not the difficult part. The difficult part is finding out whether that patent is going to be worth something. However, there is one reason obtaining a patent is a good idea, besides the protection it gives you – it shows you're serious.

One of my clients said it very well:

If it's a good idea, that's nice.

If it's a good idea and it's applicable to our business, that's better.

If it's a good idea, applicable to our business, and will actually improve our business, we might be interested.

But – *if the inventor thinks enough of his idea to actually obtain a patent,* then we must see it.

Your idea has to be good enough to draw corporate interest. Spending your own money to obtain a patent can in many cases open the door for you when a good idea all by itself could not. Hence, getting a patent is both a sales tool and a means of protection. But let's not get ahead of ourselves.

There are five ways to control an idea: You can receive a copyright, obtain a trademark, claim unfair competition, keep it as a trade secret, or get a patent. How you protect your idea really depends upon what the idea is, since not all of these ways can be applied to the same sort of idea.

Copyright

If your idea takes the form of a creative work such as a play or a song, a book or software code, then you protect it with a copyright. A copyright is used mainly to keep other people from using what you have created without your permission. Even a verse of a song is protected – a copyright covers the entire work, and even a small part of it.

The best part about a copyright is that it is yours automatically, without you doing anything more than creating that work. That protection lasts for your entire lifetime plus seventy years. This means that your heirs can benefit from your work, as well. But seventy years after your demise, the work enters the public domain and becomes available to the public at no charge.

To determine whether you need a copyright on your work, look at what makes it up. If your invention has lots of gears and levers and parts, you don't need a copyright, you need a patent. Generally, if the work can be written down, the written form gets copyrighted. So, if you invent a new type of can opener, the can opener is not protected by the copyright but the instructions on how to use it are.

Trademark

For some reason, people often confuse a trademark with a copyright, but a trademark is really simple. A trademark is a name or identifying symbol that's used in trade. Trade, mark. Get it?

For example, the Coca-Cola logo has that little ® in the lower right-hand corner of it. That means it's a registered trademark – registered with the PTO – and you can't use that name without permission. This keeps people from making something that looks like Coca-Cola and calling it Coca-Cola when in fact it's not.

If you see the letters ™ next to a name, it typically indicates the owner is claiming the name as a trademark. A trademark doesn't have to be a word; it can be a mark or a seal, as well. So, you can't use the Texaco star or Shell's seashell design on a gasoline product because it would fool the public into thinking that your product was backed by or associated with either the Chevron Products Company (Texaco's parent company) or Royal Dutch Shell.

You can claim just about anything graphical as a trademark, but to really protect it, you have to register it with the PTO. If you're the first person to register it, you get the exclusive right to use it and no one else can use it for the same purpose.

Now, watch out! You can use something that looks really close to the Texaco star on a package of bubble gum, but you can't use the exact star. If you used the Texaco star and put a similar name on the bubble gum – calling it, for instance, Taxaco – you would clearly be trying to confuse the public. It's a matter of interpretation. The court will try to determine your intent. Did you intend to confuse people to get more sales, or did you just like the design and thought it would help sales?

Unfair Competition Claim

Now, it would certainly be understandable if you get confused by this. The law distinguishes between a mark that's used for trade (a trade mark, remember) and the dress or design of the product. Well, what's the difference? I agree, it's difficult to tell them apart. The name Kodak is a registered trademark, but the shade of yellow on the box can't be used by others, either.

How would you protect that particular shade of yellow so that some low-cost film manufacturer doesn't sell "Kodax" film in a package that looks like the Kodak film box? You can't register a color. How would you protect it?

The law provides protection to keep imitators from copying the way your package looks and trying to pass off their product as yours. This is the unfair competition claim. The thrust of this is to determine the intention of the person doing the imitation. Is it just an honest similarity, or is the person trying to confuse the public?

Unfair competition claims are legal grounds for getting a judge to tell the imitator to stop. The right is inherent in the design of the trade dress, or distinctive presentation, of your product. The Walt Disney Company applies both trademark and unfair competition legal actions to protect its products. That's because Disney's products are all clever artwork. They are things that are drawn and can easily be imitated. Disney's designs are so clever that people will pay for a T-shirt emblazoned with a Disney character. After all, it's not just the T-shirt that the public is buying, it's the character. It's that design element that consumers want, so it makes sense to protect it.

Trade Secret

The formula for making Coca-Cola is a closely guarded secret, locked up somewhere in the corporate offices. And it's a secret that put Coca-Cola on the map! It gave the company domination of the soft-drink trade – it's a trade secret.

A trade secret is something that makes your product unique – generally, a flavoring, recipe, or way you make something, which you keep secret. The protection is in the secrecy. If someone can reverse engineer your product, working backward by taking the finished product and figuring out how it was made, your secret can be discovered. Then you lose it. But you can lose it another way, just by being lazy and not protecting the secret.

You must prove to the court that you took reasonable steps to keep the information secret. Every person who knows the secret has to take an oath to keep it SECRET. Every time the secret idea is written down, it is stamped secret, or at least CONFIDENTIAL. If you've made an honest effort to keep it secret and someone steals it, then the court will back you up and make him or her stop using your trade secret. But if you let just one person learn the secret and not swear to keep it secret, then you might lose it. The nice thing about a trade secret is that it's never made public. A potential competitor hasn't a clue how you make whatever it is that you make.

Patent

The four forms of protection explained above are nice to know about, but they probably don't apply to your invention if your invention is that thing we talked about that has gears and levers and wheels and such. Copyrights, trademarks, unfair competition claims, and trade secrets probably don't apply if your invention is a useful *thing* of some sort (even if it has no moving parts).

Useful things you want to sell are generally protected best by a patent. So it's worth spending a little time here explaining patents and the way they are obtained, so you can see what you have to do.

Regardless of the method of protection, sooner or later, you are going to have to be prepared to go to court to obtain enforcement. That costs money. As a matter of fact, that's what really starts to get expensive in a hurry. But patents are probably the most expensive because not only could it cost you to obtain enforcement, but also you have to pay to get a good patent properly prepared. So let's look at what a patent is and how to get the right kind.

Patents are about rights. When you invent something, you have put work into it, and if that work is unique and clever, the government acknowledges that you should be able to benefit from your work, and it issues you rights. The rights generally take the form of excluding others from using or selling what your invention is or does. That can be very valuable.

Imagine if you were the only person who could sell transistors. No one else could sell them, just you. Why, they're used everywhere! You could charge for each one. You'd be rich – very rich. That is, if you had the rights.

Well, too bad, Bell Labs beat you to it. But your turn is coming up.

There are three different kinds of patents, and each provides a different kind of protection. The three are a plant patent, a design patent, and the one you are probably most familiar with, a utility patent.

A plant patent covers plants. Now that's not too difficult to understand. It protects new plants, mainly. Scientists and companies spend really big money developing special hybrid seeds and plants. It's a laborious and tricky job. Once they have finished, they obtain patent coverage of the particular combination of characteristics so they can exclude others from growing and using these plants. The length of coverage is twenty years from the date of filing.

A design patent covers the design of something, its look. The length of coverage is fourteen years from the date you file your patent application with the patent office. Design can be very important in making sales. The unique shape of an item often is the only reason consumers choose one item over another. A design patent deals with the superficial aspects of some item – the item would still function the same way if its form were changed.

But design issues can present the unwary inventor with a serious problem. A design patent is sometimes naively bought by inventors who really should have obtained something different – a utility patent. If you get a design patent when in fact you need a utility patent, it can cost you your idea. So it's a good idea to spend some time understanding both. A design patent and a utility patent are two different legal instruments, and they protect entirely different things: Design patents cover designs; utility patents cover workings.

Here's a good way to determine whether you need a utility patent or a design patent. Take away the thing that's unique about your invention (either the shape or the workings) and see if it changes the use of the item. If taking away the workings changes the way it's used, then you need a utility patent; if it doesn't, you need a design patent. It's that simple.

For example, let's say you designed a bottle opener in the shape of a beer can. It's cute. Let's say that the shape of the beer can is the thing that is really unique. If you take away the really unique thing – in this case the beer can design – would the bottle opener still open bottles? Sure, it would. So it's the design that you want to protect. However, if you have a design patent on your beer can art and then you decide to

change the design – let's say from a beer can to a beer mug –
the beer can design patent would not cover this new beer
mug design. A design patent is therefore pretty weak. In
many cases, it can easily be designed around.

The reason patented designs are subject to a lot of chi-
canery is that design patents, being pretty weak, are relatively
inexpensive to get. It doesn't require anywhere near the kind
of documentation and thought that a utility patent requires.
But because a design patent is still a real, honest-to-goodness
United States PTO patent, some inventors mistakenly believe that if they obtain a design patent, their invention will
be protected.

That's what you often will get if you respond to those ads
in the paper that advertise cheap patents. You'll get a patent,
all right, but you might be getting the wrong kind. It's not exactly illegal to sell somebody something he or she doesn't
need or that is practically worthless, so it's difficult to stop
this practice. It's really up to the inventor to know the difference between patents and to be able to distinguish the rights
he or she wants to protect.

If it's not the design that's important but instead is the
way the product works and the way the parts move, then you
need a utility patent. That's the kind of patent most people
think of when they think of a patent. A utility patent is the
strongest, the most involved, and the most difficult patent to
get. That's because it conveys to the holder of the patent
(you) certain very valuable rights. The government says it's
OK for you to be the sole owner of this idea for a limited time
– twenty years from the date you file your application with
the patent office. The day you file, the clock starts.

But that's not when you receive the patent. It's important
to note that the filing date is different from the date the
patent is allowed. Your idea must go through a lengthy

process before the patent office decides that they can allow you those very valuable rights. There is liable to be plenty of back and forth with the patent office to get the language exactly right before they will allow a patent. It can take up to three years or more to get a patent. After you are notified that your patent is allowed, you can enforce it.

Generally, a few months after you receive notice that your patent will be granted, it will issue. The issue date is the date the patent becomes available to the general public. For some reason, the PTO does this on a Tuesday. Your patent will be published in the Patent and Trademark Office's Official Gazette, which comes out on a Tuesday.

That's it. That's all it is. You get a letter and it's published in the PTO's Official Gazette and it's a patent. You will get a letter from the PTO saying you have a patent. If you want, you can frame and hang the letter on the wall, but that letter is not the patent any more than your graduation certificate is your education. The letter is just evidence that you really have the exclusive rights to the patent. If you lose the letter, don't panic. You still have the patent. You can get another letter.

Once you have a patent, you can prevent anyone else from using the ideas you've described in the claims section of the patent. If someone uses any of the material you have put into the claims section, you can go to court and the court can issue an injunction making the other party stop. This is a very serious situation, which unfortunately happens more than you might imagine.

But let's not get ahead of ourselves. While the PTO is looking over your idea, you have the right to claim that a patent is pending. The patent itself may not issue. It may be turned down flat. But nonetheless, you can put a label or inscription on the invention that a patent is pending.

CHAPTER 9

The Utility Patent

A U.S. patent begins with a title page and a summary of what the patent describes. This description is called an abstract. The abstract is very handy because in very little space it gives an idea of what the patent covers. The title page contains other very useful information, such as the patent number, the date filed, the date issued, and the classification number. There is a lot more on the title page, but it isn't critical to our discussion.

The title page is followed by drawings, or in patent language, figures. They are all numbered, and various parts of the invention are pointed out with numbers as well. After the figures is a description of the field to which the invention belongs.

Then there is a section that presents the background of the invention. Generally, this explains why the invention was developed. That is followed by a summary of the invention, which is just a description in some detail of what your widget is and a brief description of the drawings that show the invention. That is followed by a description of the preferred embodiments. The embodiments are the way(s) the invention would probably appear.

The last part is the most important. The last part presents the claims. The claims lay out all the little pieces of the patent to which you have rights.

What? You mean a patent is a bunch of *pieces* of an idea?

Yes, the claims in total are supposed to completely describe your idea. To do that, each little aspect is claimed separately. The language used has grown up over the years as lawyers talk to lawyers, so you can imagine how complicated it can become. But let's not worry about how it's written. Let's worry about the claims themselves, because that's what gets you paid.

Now, here is a very important thing to know: You can describe your invention in exhaustive detail, but none of it will be covered by a patent if it isn't included in the claims section. That means every little aspect, every nuance, has got to be down in black and white in the claims section. If it appears anywhere else but not in the claims section, it isn't covered under the patent.

In other words, if you don't claim it, you don't get it. Got it?

When you finally get to that all-important meeting with the execs who will have the make-or-break decision about your idea in their hands, I guarantee that something like this will happen: Their lawyer or, if one of the execs is well grounded in patent law, your customer will ask to see your patent. You will hand it over. He or she won't even look at the first pages; she'll go right to the back, because at the back is the most important part of the patent – the claims. It's easy to spot. It begins, "I claim..." Then it lists everything that you claim, and that's what you have exclusive rights to. *Everything you wish to have a right to must be in the claims.* This is very important.

Very often, people show me patents that talk about a particular aspect of their invention – and it isn't covered in the claims! This can be a real tragedy. If you don't claim it in your patent, you don't own it. Period. Not only can you not claim ownership of that particular aspect but also, once the patent issues, you have just two years to file a broader version covering something that you might have missed. After that, you're stuck with what you've got. Material not covered in the claims is considered donated to the public. Once you receive the patent, it is published. Once it's published, anybody can view it. And because public information can't receive a patent, your very own patent can be used against you to keep you from claiming additional rights that are given in the descriptive part of the patent.

If any aspect of your invention is available to the general public, you can't claim it. That means any description of what it does or how it works. Now be careful here. A description of the general way an airplane might fly doesn't mean you can't patent the shape of the wing. But if a drawing of your airplane wing suddenly appears in the newspaper after you came up with it, then you have up to one year to file for your patent or it's over. You've lost it.

Any prior public exposure of your idea, or the working of your idea, is called "prior art." *Art* is the fancy word the PTO uses to describe work or tinkering in the field – no matter where the article is published. It can be Timbuktu; it doesn't matter.

It really makes sense. It prevents a crooked inventor from reading the Timbuktu *Morning Register,* and after seeing this airplane wing described, running right out and patenting it. It keeps inventors from taking other people's work and claiming it as their own. If you can view it somewhere or read about it somewhere, you can't claim patent rights to it – that is, if the medium in which you got it or read about it was publicly available.

"Publicly available" means it's where anybody can get at it. If the idea is written down and stamped CONFIDENTIAL and was stolen from your safe, and you can prove it to the court, you still may be able to patent it. That's why I stress maintaining a trail of discovery of the idea development and keeping everything confidential.

This same argument goes for selling the product. If you offer your product for sale at any time before you file for a patent, you can't claim any of the invention. The reason is just the same as seeing the idea in the Timbuktu *Morning Register*. If you see it on the Home Shopping Network, chances are lots of other people have seen it, too. Now, we can't have them all rushing down to the patent office to file patents, can we? How would the PTO tell which person had the idea first? They couldn't just give the patent to the first person that makes it through the door. Perhaps the real inventor lives far away, or perhaps the real inventor didn't even see it on TV to begin with. So offering your product for sale before you file can be tricky, and it might keep you from getting any protection from a U.S. patent.

Now, as I mentioned before, there is one exception: If your invention is published before you file for your patent but you can present evidence that you came up with the idea before it appeared in the paper (remember all those little dated and signed pieces of paper you've been meticulously protecting?), then you have one year from this publication to file, absent any other claims. Other than that single exception, anything about your invention that is in the public domain becomes prior art.

Prior art is the single most common reason patent holders lose their claims. It is a common misconception that the patent examiner will review all the previous work in the field and then, if he or she can't find your idea, give you a patent. It doesn't work that way. Patent examiners are clever and highly skilled; however, they can't know everything about a particular field. They can't read all the magazines and go to all the lectures and talk with all the customers. They've got other things to do – such as approving your patent. They don't have time for all that research. But prior art can keep you from getting a patent on the idea. So you need to find out what prior art is out there. The first place you should look is among the over seven million patents issued by the Patent and Trademark Office. If it isn't in that database, there's a good chance it isn't going to be anywhere. So here's a good rule of thumb: Do a patent search.

What exactly is a patent search? It is just what it sounds like – a search of the PTO files for something that is sort of like your idea. If you find someone else has patented some part of your idea, you must reveal it to the patent office. If you don't, and the PTO can prove that you purposely withheld that information, you can get into serious trouble.

Actually, it makes no sense at all to fail to deal with prior art references to your idea. If someone has a patent on something you wish to claim, then somewhere, at some time, you will butt heads. But if you reveal the prior art to the patent office, point out the differences between that prior art and your idea, and convince the patent examiner that your idea is different, then that other person would have no grounds to claim they had the idea. Or, to put it into PTO talk, it would be very difficult for anyone to interfere with your claims on the basis of that piece of prior art. If you were able to convince the PTO of the difference, then another inventor claiming your idea would be stopped before even getting started.

But there is still one tricky wrinkle. Prior art can be found everywhere; it is not limited to U.S. patents. There are magazines and trade journals and published letters and studies and a host of professors talking and talking about all sorts of wonderfully clever things. If your idea is described in one of these publications or presentations or is made public in any way, you're sunk, just as if it were patented by someone else.

And there are loads of foreign patents and references that might be in force in the United States.

Fortunately, you can get a good idea of the foreign patents and magazines that might predate your filing. The front page of every patent has a section called "References Cited." It's a list of patents and publications that have been reviewed prior to the allowance of the patent. If you look through the PTO files and find several patents that are in your field but that don't have the same claims, you can look at the front page of those other patents to determine what prior art might be out there, and you can then search for pieces of your idea.

Searching the patent office files for prior art used to be a real hassle. I would have to drive from my house to a university, which was a repository for the microfilm records of the PTO. I would then sit for hours at one of those microfilm readers going through all these patents. What a pain!

But in this age of cyberspace, I don't drive anywhere to research prior art. I go into my home office and push a couple of keys on my computer and search the PTO database right from the comfort of my own chair. What's more, I enter in a keyword or two and up come all the references that might apply. Now, that's modern convenience! You can do it, as well. It's easy. The PTO has a Web site that explains it all, at www.uspto.gov. (And please notice that the extension is .gov, not .com. Another company has grabbed .com because lots of folks get sloppy and forget that the PTO is a governmental agency and thus has the .gov designation.)

However, if you're still a little skeptical about doing a preliminary search on your own, go to my Web site, www.howtosellyouridea.com, and I'll walk you through it *for free*. How's that for a deal?

Now you see why I can predict with absolute certainty that your customer will flip right to the claims section of the patent, because that's really all you have for sale. Just that. All the other stuff is just prior art.

It should be clear by now that you must be pretty careful when it comes to drafting the claims of your patent. They must be as complete and tight as you can possibly make them. The difficulty is that the tighter you make them, the less you can cover. That's why you really need a patent lawyer to help you in drafting the document – and that's why a patent can cost you a lot of money. Writing the claims starts the meter running and the cash starts to flow. When you start hiring lawyers, it gets expensive. But if they're good, they'll be well worth it.

I suppose at this juncture it makes sense to give you an idea of what kind of money you might be talking about. Patent attorneys' fees vary from state to state and from law firm to law firm. It's not unusual to find patent attorneys charging two hundred to five hundred dollars an hour. The more experienced they are, the more expensive they are.

One of the ways you can spare your pocketbook is to find a young patent attorney who is eager for your business and use him for all the preliminary work. You can even let him take a crack at writing the claims. Then (and you don't have to tell him you are doing this), you should show the claims to someone more senior for a very brief read-over. He or she will charge you for one hour of time, but if they're any good, they will spot any serious flaws.

As I've said, claims writing is complicated and tricky. You want the claims well drafted, and you should be willing to spend the most money for this. After all, those claims are all you have to sell when the time comes.

Once you start writing checks for legal help, things can

start to get out of hand. Patents have a reputation for being expensive. That's because they can have great value, which means there will inevitably be arguments about exactly what area is protected and what area is not. Unfortunately, the U.S. government – and particularly the U.S. PTO – isn't going to referee any arguments that might arise between two people who both want to use some of the area covered by a patent.

This means that a patent is an invitation to a lawsuit. Just because you have a patent doesn't mean you are safe from infringement. The PTO grants patents; it does not enforce them. The enforcement is up to you, and it can get pretty expensive because now we are talking about attorneys and courts and lawsuits.

Actually, it makes sense. It is your property, not the government's, and what you do with your property is up to you.

So what do you do if someone infringes on your patent? Let's say they sit right on top of your claims and dare you to sue them. It's a bit daunting, and it puts you in a very awkward position because you must either defend your claims or give up your right to the particular claim that is being used without permission.

What? If you don't sue, you lose your patent?

Yes, I'm afraid that's about it. This, too, makes sense. If you don't enforce your rights, then the court assumes you don't care about that particular claim. Therefore, you must enforce all the claims you want to keep, and you have to sue every violator. You can't let one company get away with something and then sue another company for the same infraction. To give you some elbow room, however, you have up to six years to take action against a known infringer.

As you see, once you've secured a patent, it puts you in a constant state of possible legal action. Because patent lawsuits are the really expensive part of patent protection, this work generally is best left to large companies who have lawyers on staff to handle litigation. To try to do it yourself is very difficult.

There is a way around this particular problem, though: When you sell rights to your patent, stipulate in the licensing agreement that your customer can use the claims *as long as the customer defends the claims from possible infringement.* In other words, pass the buck

Of course, some companies will resist this. They will want you to enforce your own patent. They have a point; it *is* your responsibility. But the expense can get to be so great that a single individual can't do a very good job, so it ultimately comes down to how valuable the patent is. If it's really valuable, then your customer will be glad to defend. The company that buys the rights to your claims will look at it this way: If you are unable to mount a good defense because you can't afford a good lawyer, or if you have to drop the case because you run out of money, the company is the one that gets hurt. It will lose its protection, too. It may not want to lose that protection.

Again, the tactic of having the customer agree to defend the patent against infringement will only fly if the patent has some real value. If your patent is not all that valuable, your customer's interest will decline in proportion to the amount of value the customer can see in it.

What You Must Have to Get a Patent

There are four basic requirements your invention must have to receive a U.S. patent. Your idea must be classifiable, useful, novel, and unobvious.

YOUR IDEA MUST BE CLASSIFIABLE

This is not as silly as it sounds. The PTO has certain classification categories, and your patent must fit into one of those categories. You can see why. If it can't be classified, it can't be examined against prior patents. Classification narrows down the field of the patent to something that is easier to handle. There are some rules of thumb about this.

You'll be all right if your idea deals with a machine or a process, or even if it is a different way of using the machine or process that hasn't been thought of before. But in some cases your idea might not exactly be a machine or a process, even though it is still a unique item. What do you do then?

Your idea might then be considered a manufacture or a manufactured item. This would be something that is a whole object with no parts to it, such as a type of plastic that bounces particularly high or that has some unique character that other kinds of plastic don't have. You can see that plastic doesn't have any parts, but its composition is unique. In such a case, the item is a manufacture.

Don't let this classification thing scare you. The good news is that there are a lot of classifications, and it's the PTO's responsibility to assign your invention to a particular classification. Nonetheless, it's an important decision, because the classification will determine what other prior art and previous patents will be searched.

YOUR IDEA MUST BE USEFUL

This should be obvious. What you want are claims with useful rights. If the invention wasn't useful, why would you want exclusive rights to the uses? Where it gets tricky is that, very often, frivolous or silly items get patented. The concept of usefulness doesn't mean serious or even uplifting; it just means the idea has to have a definable use. So a doll that wets itself is perfectly patentable even if it is not particularly useful in splitting the atom or controlling long-distance power transmission. If it has a use, it qualifies.

YOUR IDEA MUST BE NOVEL

This can be tricky. "Novel" doesn't mean the first one on the block to do something that has not been done before. It just means the idea must be different from all the other types of things that do what your invention also can do. You have to be able to tell the ideas apart. This is where the prior art concept is useful. If there is prior art, then what your invention does might already be disclosed, or it might be in the public domain and therefore not claimable. But you still can get a patent. In such a case, the claims would include not what the invention did but perhaps aspects of how it did it. If those aspects are unique, you can proceed with getting your patent.

So you can get a patent on that beer-can-shaped can opener we talked about before. Perhaps it just opens beer cans and bottles, and at first glance you might think that you couldn't get a patent because, after all, lots of openers will do that. But if your opener has a unique way of doing it, you can patent that. If you get a patent on that unique method, then you can sell that aspect of the invention and get royalties just as if you had invented the beer can opener in the first place.

YOUR IDEA MUST BE UNOBVIOUS

I suspect that *unobvious* is a PTO word. The PTO likes to describe things in unusual ways like this. *Unobvious* means that the idea is not obvious to someone who would understand it if he or she saw it – that is, to someone who worked in the business or trade. The PTO calls this person "one skilled and familiar with the art" (see what I mean about archaic phrases?). In this case, the art is the task that your invention does.

The reason the PTO wants someone familiar with the art as the test of the idea's unobviousness is because patents sometimes get quite arcane. Certain fields are so complex that you have to be a real expert to understand what a particular invention does. Perhaps you or I would be floored by this invention, but someone in the field would laugh at how obvious it was. When you reach this level of complexity, it is pretty easy to come up with an idea that might seem to be very original and therefore very marketable but that would still seem pretty obvious to an expert in the field. In that case, you can sell it, you just won't be able to patent it.

Most of the difficulties in getting a patent occur as a result of this basic requirement to be unobvious. The examiner will refer to an earlier patent and say that your idea could have been figured out by relying on this earlier art; therefore, it isn't unobvious. Or, to put it another way, it is obvious.

Generally, an examiner will make this decision because he or she doesn't understand the subtle and clever differences you have designed into your idea. It's your job to point out those subtle and clever differences. It is also your job to make sure those subtle and clever differences are put in the claims! So there is always a lot of back-and-forth argument going on between the examiner, who is trying to understand all the nuances of your idea, and you, who are trying to point out how different your idea is from the ideas of all these other people who filed before you. This argument usually plays out through the U.S. mail. How well you do that job, and how convincing you are, will determine which claims you get and which ones you don't.

PART III

Presenting Your Idea

CHAPTER 10

Preparing Your Presentation

So far, you've been doing all this work to get to the point where you can take your wonderful widget and sell it to somebody. If you have done all your homework, you should be in really good shape to present a convincing case. After all,

- we've analyzed our product;
- we know its strengths and have done what we can to shore up its weaknesses;
- we've built a paper trail to establish ownership;
- we've studied the industry, so we know the market;
- we've looked at our product through our potential customers' eyes, so we know what they want and need; and
- we've gotten legal protection of some sort.

We're ready to take our wonderful widget out into the wide world and sell it to someone. Now we have to set up a meeting with one of the players in the field. This is far and away the most important part of this entire process. If you can get through this next meeting and they ask you back for more discussions, you will have a chance at selling this product. If it's going to sell, it will happen here.

But this also is where most products get stopped cold, so we need to take this very seriously. This is your first and your last chance. You can't afford to miss anything in preparing to pitch your idea at this meeting. As we've already discussed, your potential customers are going to be looking your idea over very carefully, so you have to have everything in order.

Thanks to all our preparation, we have a number of facts about the industry and the product already at hand. You now put all that information into a presentable form. It makes no difference whether you are pitching to a funding source for a business you're starting up, pitching to a company to buy your idea, or starting a partnership with a manufacturer. Now is the time to draw up a business plan.

A business plan is the way any good businessperson evaluates a product. It's sort of the common language that businesspeople use in talking to one another. If you come into that first meeting without a business plan, the executives at the meeting will know they are dealing with an amateur, and that can hurt you.

Although some plans can be very extensive and complicated, the one you will need should not be. Your business plan should be brief and simple. It should very clearly tell someone who knows very little about your idea everything he or she will need to know. Actually, it's pretty obvious. You need to tell them

- what your product is,
- the history of the field,
- the size and promise of the field,
- how your product could be made and sold,
- what profits to expect, and
- what it will take to bring the product to market.

We have already gathered all this information as we analyzed the product, so now is the time to make sure we put it down in a clear and concise manner. Bear in mind that this is your selling tool. So although you must stick to the facts, the business plan should be written in a very upbeat and positive

way. It should stress all the benefits your product can provide. In some cases it will seem obvious that, if a company
uses your idea, it will save money or make money because
your idea is better than something the company currently
has. Nonetheless, be sure to say so!

Every point you can possibly make should be in that
presentation. It's a game like tennis and you're rolling up a
score. Each benefit is a point for you. The more points you
make, the closer you are to success. Of course, you also
must stick closely to the facts and not start wildly exaggerat-
ing the size of the market or the amount of return. You are
talking to experts here and they will spot an exaggeration as
if it had lights around it.

A business plan is your plan to sell your idea. That's it. No
MBA needed. Frequently, I can put together a business plan
for an invention in about ten pages. There are a variety of
outline forms available – including software available at office supply stores or online – so you can pick the one you like.

I use the following format as an outline (you can use
something different, but do use something):

COVER SHEET: Something simple, with a discreet
copyright notice in small type at the bottom. Indicate
CONFIDENTIAL somewhere upon it. If you have a
patent or have applied for a patent, either present the
patent number or say "patent pending." None of this
has to be a screaming headline. Keep it simple, small,
and tasteful.

TABLE OF CONTENTS: List all the sections and the
pages that follow the outline you are using.

CONCEPT DISCLOSURE: State briefly what your invention does. This is a summary, not a blow-by-blow

description. The disclosure section focuses your client on the topic and the use.

EXECUTIVE SUMMARY: I've heard it said that this is the only thing any customer ever reads in a business plan, because all the rest is guesswork. It probably is true to a large extent. If they like your idea, they will rework all your numbers. But that doesn't mean you shouldn't take a stab at nailing down many of the above topics. The executive summary should deal briefly with the concept – and mainly with the money. Look into the future and try to predict the potential return in one year, five years, and ten years. Depending upon the field and the impact of your idea on that field, it can get pretty tricky to guess what the industry will look like in ten years, so touch on it but don't lean on it.

DESCRIPTION OF CONCEPT: Introduce the idea with a few sentences and then include the following subpoints:

- BACKGROUND: How the field got to where it is now.
- PLACE WITHIN THE FIELD: Where the customer's product stands in relation to yours, where their competition's product stands, and the size of the market.

MARKET POTENTIAL: This is the most important element in any business plan. This is where you must make it seem worth the customer's while. Tell them why your idea is better, and note the weaknesses of competing products. Here's where you describe what protection and patents you have already obtained and what you have applied for. Give them an idea of the steps you have taken to protect their investment.

GETTING TO MARKET: You can't have all these answers, and they will know it. Don't try to tell them their business. If you don't know how much equipment will cost, use the word *assuming,* as in, "Assuming that you use your present equipment, only a minor change will be needed in the packaging." Give them an idea of what you imagine will be needed to reach their market. Show where their present distribution can be useful. Try to use as many of their present marketing connections as possible. Try to be realistic.

This section could contain the following general topics; however, not all of them will apply to all ideas:

- Promotion and sales of concept
- Manufacturing and production considerations
- Raw materials (if applicable)
- Availability and variability of materials
- Cost of materials
- Cost of assembly and delivery (if applicable)
- Cost of the equipment to make the product
- Number of people the manufacturing will tie up

PROFIT ANALYSIS: Once again, you might not be able to fully flesh this out, but the section could include the competition's pricing and your suggested pricing. If your idea has a built-in cost savings or increase in efficiency, be sure to point that out here.

DECISIONS NEEDED: This is the action section. It's important to tell your customer what needs to be done and get them moving forward. I try to establish deadlines and commitments here. Be realistic in laying these deadlines down, however. They have a business to run while they are considering your product. No one is going to drop everything and stop the production line to analyze your widget. However, two weeks seems reasonable for at least a follow-up call on most products.

As in most things, be sure you have the responsibility for making the follow-up call. Don't wait for them. Never wait for them. If you suddenly become passive and start waiting for them to get moving, you will wait forever.

They need to make some decisions, so give them time to make them. But let them know that while they are collectively stroking their chins you will be making additional sales calls to their competition across the street. If they want you to hold off on those calls, this is the time to suggest that they offer a retainer or purchase an option on the idea. A little cash will entice you to hold your horses. But make sure that the retainer does not commit you to anything more than a stated amount of time delay. Nothing about rights, ownership, or commitments of any kind.

DEADLINES: This section may not be necessary if it is already covered under the "Decisions needed" section. However, in certain cases a company needs to know that a window of opportunity might be closing and that they must make a decision before it does. If you are offering them the rights to a product that must be sold on a seasonal basis, remind them of that deadline here.

NEXT STEPS: I always put this in any communication that calls for action from a company. You use it to do their thinking for them. Most companies have a million things going on simultaneously. You need to make it clear what they must do and when they must do it. I always keep the responsibility for these steps in my hands. I call to remind them that they must do such and such. I call to make sure that the testing is being carried out on schedule. I use this section as an excuse to keep following up. Follow up at every opportunity, to keep the pressure up and get a decision.

However, keeping after them and pushing them around are two different things. If you make yourself a pest, they will find you very irritating. In general, that is not a good idea. However, if they are particularly intransigent you might need to push harder. This is a judgment call.

Must you use this form for your presentation? Absolutely not. But make sure you use something to organize your presentation. A business plan can do the organizing for you. It gives your presentation a backbone to build around. And no matter what form you use, you must include the right kind of information.

CHAPTER 11

Getting in the Door

W hen you have your business plan about half finished, you need to start looking for a customer. I say "half finished" because some sections of the plan will be customized to the client you pick. Your plan isn't going to be universal; each client needs to feel it's been made up for them alone.

But just between the two of us, much of it can be generic. So you need to do both at about the same time. Writing the plan is a matter of organization, and finding a customer is, too. Here's what I mean.

First, you look at your market analysis and decide who would be interested in your product. If you're not sure, think of a similar product and where you saw it. If, say, it's a hardware product, then take a trip to your local home-supply store and find something similar. Then write down the manufacturer's name.

I find that many beginners confuse the manufacturer with the distributor or retailer. The company that actually makes the product is probably different from the place where you buy it. If you bought a hammer from Home Depot, it doesn't necessarily mean that Home Depot would be interested in making a new hammer. Home Depot, Wal-Mart, and Sears are retailers and distributors. Often they will have house brands that are sold under their name, but their primary business is retail and distribution.

Approaching a retailer or distributor is the toughest way to get your item manufactured and sold. You want a manufac-

120

turer. That means a company that has the equipment to build whatever it is that you have designed, because that's the business they are in. So how do you find a likely prospect?

Put your trip to the home-supply store to good use. Read boxes, packages, and anything that has a name on it. Find out who made this. Write down the name. Don't just take down one manufacturer's name. Go through all the items that are similar to your idea and repeat the process until you have a bunch of names. Now you have a list of potentially interested prospects.

Next, go to the department manager and tell them you want to contact the manufacturer. They probably have the contact information or a buyer who does. Often they will give you the manufacturers' phone numbers or Web sites. Armed with that information, you can start prospecting for potential clients.

Obviously, if you have an invention in a particular field, you do a search on the Internet. Just enter the name of something similar to what the product does or something it is similar to (airplane wing or hammer) and up come the names of all kinds of things, processes, and, mainly, makers of something like what you have in mind. From there, it's just a matter of reading. Lots of it.

These Web sites are a regular bonanza of information. First, look at all the other products the maker manufactures. See if any of what they already have duplicates anything that your widget does. If they do, this might lessen the appeal of your product. Notice government approvals or endorsements by respected associations, such as the FDA, AMA, or FCC. Can your product get the nod from these same groups?

Their product might have been submitted to and approved by various guilds, associations, and standards-setting groups. Do you think yours will be able to pass muster as theirs did?

Examine each Web site in detail. Look for personnel to contact. You'll often find names of the major department heads under a contact link. If the company Web site doesn't specify contacts, check to see if there is more than one related company under a single umbrella. For example, Oreo cookies are made by Nabisco, but Nabisco has lots of products besides Oreos. You want the name of the marketing guru for Oreo, not for the entire company. At some point, you might be in the big boardroom with the senior vice president of marketing, but probably not until several others have signed off on your idea. More often than not, a really large company will have a director of new product development or R & D. That might be a good place to start.

By the way, that first contact should be by telephone. E-mails from outside inventors are ignored. As we learned in the section on protecting your idea, any contact with an outside inventor will probably be done under an NDA. It's a big deal to get into a meeting with a large company, so don't expect them to sweep you in and sit you down without a little effort on your part. That's why phone contact is best. You can talk to someone and describe what it is that you have. They will then direct you to the appropriate person. Sometimes the best way to thread this particularly complicated needle is just to call customer service or even the main phone number and let the switchboard operator figure it out.

The realities of selling any idea are that it takes work. Lots of it. That's because people are busy and you are going to be just one more interruption in their already too-busy day. So expect lots of calls that get you nowhere. That doesn't mean you won't sell your idea. It means that you have to approach getting a client in an organized and realistic manner.

Here are a few things to bear in mind as you go about the lonely and frustrating job of getting that all-important meeting.

1. It takes ten calls to get just one prospect whose people will take the time to see you. Expect them not to be interested. It's normal. It's not a sign that there's anything wrong with your idea. Many companies don't take ideas from the outside. Many won't sign NDAs. Some are just not interested.

2. Keep very good records of everyone you talk with and every meeting you attend. This will help you recall where you are in the sales process and who you've already seen. Keep those records up to date.

3. Keep a list by your telephone of the companies you want to contact, and work through them methodically. If you start hopping around from client to client, soon you will forget which company you are meeting with and what you said.

4. Make a separate file for each customer. Keep the file active until a decision is reached. If you fail in getting a meeting, keep the file in a suspended state for six months and then try again. People move around like crazy in the business world. It's musical chairs. In six months you might have a whole new team in there. A simple phone call to the switchboard will tell you if the old VP of marketing is there or has been promoted or is gone. If nothing has changed since your last call, don't go any further.

5. Try to schedule several presentations, one after the other. If one blows up, get two more. This way, you are always moving forward. But don't necessarily schedule several presentations on the same day. This can get you

into a bind. If a meeting is going really well and you run out of time because you have another presentation, you might end up losing both customers. Much depends upon the idea, the industry, and the time it will take to explain what you have.

6. Prepare a thirty-second capsule presentation that you can leave on voice mail. Follow the who, what, when, where, and why sequence that newspapers use, but add a good bit of enthusiasm. Remember that you are selling your product, so stress the benefits and the ease of implementation. However, this little sales pitch must include enough concrete facts to give the client a chance to determine whether they are at all interested. Make it short, pithy, and engaging.

There is a very good chance that the person you want is not in the office or at their desk. Invariably, they are somewhere else. The thirty-second pitch will at least get their attention. Always include a callback schedule. That means a statement such as, "I'll try calling you again on Wednesday the tenth at one o'clock." A specific statement setting up a phone meeting can improve your chances of actually talking to the right person. If they are not there to take your call, don't get discouraged. You have no idea how busy they are. Wednesday at one might be the exact time the entire department has a weekly business review. They are trying to be organized too, you know.

Also, don't make the mistake of trying to read between the lines of their lack of response to your call. It's futile. Keep in mind that your widget is precious to you and it may become precious to them, but they don't know anything about it yet. So they can't very well get as excited about it as you are. New inventors invariably become discouraged because they guess at what should be happening when in fact they don't have any idea of what might actually be happening.

You don't know that they aren't interested just because they aren't banging on your door pleading to have a look at your widget. They are busy. You are one of many. They can't ignore you forever, so they probably aren't trying to now.

You won't actually know anything about how good your idea is until you present it to a number of people and get a consistent reaction. One person's opinion is not a final judgment. One person who doesn't return your phone call isn't an opinion at all. So don't get depressed or dramatic about their slow response. Getting meetings takes time. A lot of time. It takes time to make these calls, but it also takes their time to have to set up a meeting with you. In some cases, they have to contact several people, all of whom are busy and all of whom must drop whatever it is they do and come to your meeting. Your customer isn't about to do that lightly.

7. For goodness sake, keep trying. The quickest way to fail is to quit trying. The quickest way to succeed is to get out there and push.

CHAPTER 12

Making the Presentation

You might have put together a thorough report packed with figures and calculations proving that your idea will be a major seller. But what good will this report do if no one bothers to read it very closely? In a meeting, they won't. And even if they do glance at it, they're not going to remember what they read. The truth is, they will only remember what you tell them and what they see during the presentation. Perhaps this explains why so many ideas fail to get sold.

Most inventors make the same mistake. They think their presentation is made on paper, so logically enough (so they surmise), the prettier the paper package, the better the chances of sealing the deal. They have this mental picture of their wonderful idea all dressed up in a nice binder, with color photos and graphs and charts and tabs on every section, being passed around a table.

It's comforting, and a good idea as well, to logically spell out all your selling points and arguments in a reasoned presentation illustrated with graphs, charts, and testimonials. It sounds great, but it won't really sell your product. There's a very simple reason. No one will read your beautiful little pile of paper. No one has time to read things. And if it's not read, no one will know about all the terrific reasons and facts and testimonials.

You could write a real page-turner of a presentation and have no one ever take the time to do more than flip through it and admire how neat and thorough you are. But if you don't tell them how terrific your product is, if you don't burn into their heads how wonderful your product will be for their business, if you don't make eyeball-to-eyeball contact with them and watch their heads go up and down in agreement, they won't even know you presented it.

As far as I'm concerned, print only substantiates, it does not motivate. But you need to inspire motivation at this initial meeting. Someone in that meeting (besides yourself) has got to say to the rest of the room, "Say, this is a great idea." That's why you will craft your presentation around you and your idea, not around what you write down in a report.

You know what actually happens the minute they leave that meeting? They go back to their desks with your beautifully documented and lovingly put-together presentation in their hands and then they toss it into their in-boxes. Those boxes contain all the other stuff they are going to read, someday. Then they check voice mails and e-mails. And they never think about your little idea again.

Your audience is just like you. They're human. They're already overloaded with work. Just like you, they have to complete their regular job, and to expect them to also consider adding your idea into the mix is asking a lot. Every job has deadlines, crises and politics, phone calls and e-mails to answer. And what's more, employees have lives outside of work. Your idea doesn't rank very high compared to the doctor's appointment and the kid's braces.

You must give them a reason to remember your idea and leave them with a big itch to dig into it. You have to use this meeting to kindle a flame that will burn long after you have gone. You have to present your idea in such a bright light that they will *have* to take action on it.

Then, when they are thinking about the kid's braces, your idea will pop into their mind and they'll remember that they said, "Say, that's a great idea!"

To leave them with a big itch requires your presentation to be visually exciting and memorable. Now, before you groan and hold your head in your hands, complaining that this sounds like you're going to have to develop a vaudeville routine, relax. Yes, you have to entertain them, but I'm not suggesting that you take out chain saws and juggle them.

I simply mean you must give them a dramatic example of how your product works or what its benefits are. While you're describing the idea for the first time, present it in a compelling way. Capture the excitement and passion you feel about your invention and pass it along.

The following is a hypothetical example. We'll call it "Hot Pizza/Cold Pizza."

Let's say you have an idea for a new graphite-based paper product (we'll call it Graphizol) and you want to sell it to a manufacturer. Let's say one of the product's special qualities is its ability to keep food hot much longer than cardboard can, and you have devised a new Graphizol package for pizza. The package also costs less to make than the standard cardboard box and is easy to manufacture with the equipment on hand.

Now, this is the presentation you have sweated to obtain. You've done all this research and have gotten just the right folks all together in one room. This is D-day. This is the payoff. How are you going to sell Graphizol in such a way that those folks are going to walk out of the conference room and ten minutes later remember your presentation? Let's begin at the beginning: How would you put all those goodies about Graphizol into a concise statement?

You could write something like, "The application of Graphizol to the pizza industry will provide a number of benefits. Due to the molecular structure of the material, tests have shown that the insulation properties are much greater than that of standard paper or cardboard (see graph). This has resulted in a container that retains heat four times as long as prior materials and that costs less (see chart). In mathematical terms, the heat coefficient of Graphizol yields a significant improvement over standard cardboard (see formula)."

Is this product-summary sheet interesting? Yes, to someone in manufacturing. But is it dramatic? No!

When you present, you want to show your idea's benefits in an easy-to-understand and dramatic way. To do so requires that you dramatize the difference between your material and other kinds of material. How?

Here's one way: Borrow a technique from the newspaper industry. Newspapers have to sell you a paper every day. Every day, they have to have something that will grab you. In the old days, they would hire a bunch of kids with freckles and pug noses to stand on street corners with a dozen newspapers under their arms and yell, "Extra! Extra! Read all about it." Newspapers made the news exciting by promising something brand new and so interesting it required an extra edition.

How do you apply that hype to Graphizol, the stuff with a molecular structure that holds heat four times better than standard paper? You walk into that meeting with two pizzas – one hot, in a Graphizol box, and one cold, in a standard box. Hand out slices, and then ask, "Now, which one would you want? Hot pizza, right? Well, ladies and gents, here's your chance. The revolution has finally come. No more cold pizza. Hallelujah!

"Graphizol outperforms paper and cardboard four to one in standard heat-retention tests. Boxes made of Graphizol allow pizza to remain hot for more than two hours, compared to thirty minutes for paper. This product will solve the cold pizza problem. Your company will be unique in the industry. Imagine hot delivered pizza – all the time!"

Now, they did not realize there was such a thing as the Cold Pizza Problem. How could they? You just discovered it. What a scoop! That's what newspapers do every day. You didn't know there was an ozone hole and that it was expanding until the news media told you about it. My goodness, the ozone hole is expanding! Front-page news! "Scientists Sound Alarm on Expanding Ozone Hole!" Now, the ozone hole may expand every year. It might be a completely normal event. But no readers would buy a paper if it was perfectly normal, would they?

See what I mean? On the train at night, going home, what will that brand manager think about? The kid's braces, of course. But then he'll smile as he remembers the hot and cold pizza. He's never seen anything like Graphizol. The demonstration was entertaining – and convincing.

Now, how do you make sure you stay on track to keep their interest?

First, write down all the sales points of your idea. List them in a logical order. Generally, the who, what, when, where, why, and how approach works well. Make believe that you are writing a newspaper article or script for a newscaster. Lead with the most dramatic thing first: "No more cold pizza." After all, that's what this product, Graphizol, is all about.

Follow up with secondary points of somewhat lesser impact:

- Outperforms paper and cardboard

- Less expensive than other materials
- Easily made with present equipment

As you write your presentation outline, think about all the various departments that are going to have an interest in your product. Manufacturing is going to want to know how difficult it will be to make your widget, so be sure to say during your presentation, "Easily made with your present equipment."

What would Sales want? "Less wasted pizza. Happy customers."

What about R & D? "Outperforms paper and cardboard."

If you need extra help in fashioning a dramatic, concise, catchy presentation, you may want to seek professional assistance. Selling products is complicated. You need to know what will be going on in this meeting and how to determine who is important and who is just along for the ride. You need to read the client and determine how they are reacting to your sales pitch. Here's a somewhat superficial look at several of the things you will need to know.

As you organize your presentation, keep in mind that your first meeting must lead to your second, and your third, and so forth. You aren't just presenting once–that is, we hope you will pass the initial test. In the first meeting you must motivate them to want you to come back a second time to meet with more of the staff. If there is no interest in your idea during the first meeting, there is no point in having a second one. So, don't hold back on the first meeting. Make it dramatic, entertaining, interesting, and hopefully, short.

Why short? You must think about your presentation from the client's point of view. These executives are making room for you in their daily calendar because you sound like you know what you're talking about, you have an interesting idea that they need to hear about, or they don't want you to go to their competition without first knowing what you have. That's why you got in. They are taking time to meet with you to do only one thing: to either take you in or take you out – that is, to disqualify you. You must make the cut at the first meeting. So pull out all the stops for this one. Tease them with a taste. Hook them with a dramatic opening. Answer all their questions. Then, end it!

If you carry on too long and in too much depth during that first meeting, you are giving them too much detail. That just gives them more information to pick apart. It's a real fine line you're walking. You must give them enough information so they can make a valid decision, of course, but don't go into exhaustive detail. Give them the juicy parts, not all the nitty-gritty.

Consider the previews you see in the theater. They don't put the slower-moving sections in the trailer, do they? The studio is selling something to you. They put in all the action parts, the parts that move or stimulate or arouse curiosity. That's because they want you to come back and see this new movie. You must do the same with your idea.

Short sentences. Dramatic situations. And an easily remembered line of dialogue: "No more cold pizza!" If you have a good outline and a dramatic way of presenting the benefits, you likely are a long way down the road toward delivering an outstanding, exciting, winning presentation, one that will gain momentum for your idea within the company's chain of command.

No matter to whom you are presenting, there are several things you must do to keep the idea growing and moving forward. Remember, without your presence, your idea is like a satellite without the booster rocket. It might have enough velocity to make it into orbit or it might not. Anything you can do to keep it moving is beneficial.

Above all else, your idea must maintain momentum. I have seen so many really terrific ideas just peter out from lack of follow-through. Companies are busy – at least, the ones you present to had better be – and busy companies have lots going on. Your idea is just one more log on the pile, and you have to keep it at the top of the pile. The simplest way to do that is to keep reminding the people who can help your idea that they need to get behind it. You must constantly follow up and keep it moving.

Here is a vital rule for pushing your project forward in the meetings stage: As you end your presentation, tell them what step they need to take next. It gets them moving forward. Remember, you did this in the business plan you wrote. Now you do it again, but this time verbally, and get them to agree. Once you have them taking the first step, the second is a lot easier, and the third is easier still.

In a busy firm, there are so many things going on all the time that it's easy to forget what was said and what was agreed upon. To keep everyone on the same page, I always write a conference report of every meeting I have. A conference report is like the minutes of the meeting. What happened, who said what, and what was agreed upon.

If it's a telephone meeting, I write a telephone conference report. If it's a formal presentation, I write a formal meeting conference report. I list everyone at the meeting and what they do. I try to recall what everyone said, and what they liked and didn't like. I try to capture on paper what went on.

That conference report will keep you and everyone else clear on what was accomplished and what still has to be done. Most importantly, it will help you follow up.

On the next page is an example of the kind of conference report I write.

A conference report like this will refresh everyone's memory on the next step. Often, the client will prepare a conference report, as well. This is a very good idea when a project is particularly complicated or when several people have tasks to bring to the group. A comparison of reports will reveal any misunderstandings and clarify who is doing what. And I always end my conference report with a "next step." That means putting in writing what should happen next. If it doesn't happen when it is supposed to, you can follow up. Be sure to include hard dates in that conference report. Don't just say "next week" or "next month" or, worse yet, "when next we meet." Be specific.

A conference report gives you an excuse to follow up in a courteous manner and to remind people of their responsibility for the upcoming meeting. Needless to say, it also keeps control of the forward momentum of the project in your hands. Although no piece of paper is going to assure that your project stays on track, regular follow-up will at least keep you informed of where the bottlenecks are.

"Say, Bill, how's that profit analysis coming? You remember we agreed you were going to have it by Friday. Is there anything you need from me to help you get it done by then?"

Send a conference report to everyone you think would need it. This keeps everyone informed on the progress of the idea and aware of when deadlines are coming up. I sometimes send corrections, changes, or follow-up reports as the project moves along. The idea is to make it clear enough in the write-up so that someone new could read it and be instantly up to speed on what is happening and why.

CONFIDENTIAL

CONFERENCE REPORT

Acme Corp HQ
1234 Clark St., Baltimore, MD 2nd floor conference room
2–15–06

WHO: Bill Smith — VP Sales Promotion, Sue Jones — Sales,
Josephine Torelli — Sales, Al Ricardo — Legal, Clint Potter — Prod

WHAT: Widget Patent

This is to summarize the meeting held with Bill Smith, VP of Sales Promotion, and staff at Acme Corp HQ in Baltimore. Acme expressed interest in acquiring nonexclusive rights to U.S. Pat 5,123,567 — An Exhaust Means for Internal Combustion Engines (aka Widget). Mr. Kamille discussed applications and a summary of the extent of the coverage with special emphasis on Claims 2–6. Clint Potter of Production discussed the fabrication materials — steel is cheaper, aluminum is lighter. It was decided that aluminum would work. Sue Jones of Sales pointed out that pricing was a serious concern in the field and strongly suggested a fabrication method be found to reduce overall pricing by at least 20 percent. Mr. Potter and Mr. Philips of Production will investigate and report to the group on Wednesday.

NEXT STEP: The same group will meet next Wednesday at 3 in HQ 202 to review progress and begin license discussion. Mr. Kamille is to present terms. He is to bring his own legal representative. Al Ricardo will attend to represent the company. Mr. Potter will prepare a production schedule. The meeting ended at 4:20.

Distribution: ACME B Smith — VP Sales Promotion, S Jones — Sales, J Torelli — Sales, A Ricardo — Legal, C Potter — Prod. S Kamille — CEO Longview Corp.

It is up to you to keep your idea moving through the pipeline.

Think of your idea like a well-prepared meal. As you present it and immediately afterward, it will appear hot and tasty and desirable. Once you leave the conference room, however, it will start to cool. That's because you are the one putting in all the heat, the interest, and the enthusiasm. If your energy is the reason the idea is appealing, then once you leave, the idea will start to lose its appeal. It will cool off. As it cools, more and more problems will appear. Finally, the idea will start to disappear. Then, when you call, they will have almost forgotten about it.

But if the idea has merit, they will start to provide some of the heat needed to keep it appetizing. The better they like it, the more heat they will put into it and the hotter it will be. If they really like it, they will discuss it without you. This is the best of all possible worlds. They are taking the idea inside and making it part of their company.

If they start to internalize your idea, you are very near to a sale. Each department will add its input and the idea will really start to grow. At some point, someone is going to feel confident enough about the idea to take it up the chain. Depending on the idea and the level of interest, it could go all the way to the top and get approved.

Failing that, they might take it forward and collect all the negatives that upper management comes up with. Then they will bring those problems back to you for a solution.

Oddly enough, they will not try to solve these problems themselves. They will wait for you. In their minds, you are the expert. It's your idea. You have the ownership. Until they own it, they will not solve any of the problems. So you will go through a round of new questions and come up with new, pithy, and exciting answers. This might happen several times. Don't get discouraged, because each round of questions rolls you a little closer to a sale. After a bit, you will find that the company starts to engage in the trip. You will pick up allies with ideas and helpful suggestions.

Launching any new product is an exciting adventure, because a new product covers new terrain. It involves new types of challenges and new puzzles to solve. Companies are equipped to handle just those sorts of challenges. They do that every day. Now you are asking them to use their resources to solve the challenges your product will create. And they will.

They will, if it's worth their while. They will, if they believe that you understand what you're up against. They will, if they believe you know what you're talking about and have scouted out the territory already. They will commit if you convince them that you know the road ahead and can get them over the hills.

But that means you must really know as much about this product and its market as can reasonably be expected. After all, you are coming to them because you want to work with them in this new area; you'd better know that new area, and know it well. They certainly won't commit their resources to someone who has a clever idea and not a clue about the market that idea is going to be used in.

You should bear in mind that they want a partner, not a peddler. If they buy your idea, they are also going to be buying your expertise about your idea. And you have to make them feel that you are going to be a welcome addition to their already overburdened staff.

This is not to say that you should exaggerate your skills or overstate how easy it will be to get over the inevitable obstacles. They know the business and will know when you're stretching the truth. But you can make it very clear that you aren't going to create any new obstacles and that you are going to bend over backward to do whatever you can to help them with the ones you will jointly face. It is in your own best interest. It's an investment in your future.

There is something you must realize when you are at that first presentation and the forces are gathered: The people in that meeting aren't inventors. As a matter of fact, most of them aren't very creative. You're the guy with that unique gift. It's rare. It's so rare that they will admire it, but they won't know what to do with it. What seems clear to you is absolutely opaque to them. They just don't think the way you do. So you have to make an effort to show them the same thing that you see, and it might be hard for them at first.

In fairness, you have to look at it from their point of view. They already have a profitable business Why should they suddenly start selling something new that *might* make money, or then again, might not? CEOs don't become CEOs by taking chances. They have to believe, just as you do. It's up to you. It's your job to make them believers.

CHAPTER 13

Closing the Deal

After that first meeting, you either will be on the way to closing the deal or on the way out the door. If you are going to close, you will be asked for another meeting, and then another, and so on. Finally, at some point the meetings will come to an end and the final part will begin. However, just because there are no more meetings doesn't mean you will close the sale.

Some companies have very conservative people in key places. That can cause you a lot of trouble if you aren't wary. The company itself might be ideal, but if you run into a manager who isn't very aggressive you can find yourself spinning your wheels. This won't show up until it comes time to talk about the contract. Then a weak manager will delay. Up to that point things will go swimmingly because it's not real. Once a commitment has to be made there will be an abrupt change. You have to be alert for this if you want to get them to sign the contract.

I remember quite well visiting one of the leading companies in its field and talking with the senior vice president of research and development. Now, this was a pretty senior position, because this company was very research intensive. Frankly, I thought that this guy was the key to getting his company to buy several of my patented ideas. Not only had he expressed interest in my patents but also he seemed to respond quite well to my understanding of his business.

I knew I was doing well because at around 11 a.m. he said,

"Say, Stu, are you free for lunch? I'd like to spend some more time discussing this with you."

Needless to say, that was music to my ears. I quickly agreed and then made an excuse to duck out to the men's room, where I called my secretary and canceled my prior lunch date and 1 p.m. meeting. Then, all smiles, the senior VP and I continued our chat, talking amiably about the industry and my view of things. He told me about his company and where things were headed. I thought we were going to be great friends. Finally, at around 11:45 he called in his director of development and the three of us went off to lunch.

Wow, I thought I had hit the mother lode! In my experience, it's rare when a busy, high-level executive can, on the spur of the moment, change his lunch plans. To me it signaled a sincere interest.

I was wrong.

It isn't that we didn't have a great lunch and a cozy chat. It isn't that the director of development wasn't equally pleasant. It's just that, although this senior VP always accepted my calls and often met me for lunch, I never sold anything. He acted very interested. He said all the right things. I kept trying to close, but he always nodded his head and then said something like, "You're right. We should get control of this. I'll mention it to my legal department and they'll contact you. Now, as we were discussing..."

Dumb me. It took me nearly a month to realize that our lunch dates were going nowhere. Yes, I heard from his lawyers. Yes, we discussed terms. But the negotiations just dragged on and on and on. There was never a definitive moment when I could tell the deal was going to close. We must have gone through seven rewrites of the contract, and each time another issue would surface.

That should have been a warning to me. If new issues are constantly arising, then someone isn't doing his homework. After a time it became clear that they would keep massaging this agreement forevermore. I couldn't get beyond the first draft to a nearly complete second draft before another problem would crop up. Then we would start all over again.

Finally, I gave my first contact, the senior VP of R & D, a call and put it directly to him: "Mr. – – , we have been negotiating for about six weeks now, and frankly, I don't think we are making the kind of progress I had hoped. If you really want this, then I suggest you speak with your lawyers about winding it up."

"Of course," he said. "You're right about that. I'll speak to them directly. I can't see why we can't get this wound up before Christmas."

And then the merry-go-round started all over again. Christmas came and went. New Year's came and went. Then he was overseas. Then he was drawing up the new budget. Then there was a big conference he had to attend.

Finally, I looked back at my calendar and realized I had been working on this agreement for several months and was still no nearer to having a final agreement than after that first lunch. As much as I hated to admit it, I finally saw that I was never going to get an agreement. It wasn't that my contact wasn't sincere. He was perfectly sincere. He was just incapable of committing to the deal. He only managed problems, he didn't solve problems. He couldn't commit himself, finally, to a piece of paper.

Every time I called with a hard deadline, he would talk himself around it. Every time I said this deal was dead, he would find a reason to keep the deal alive. Finally, I quit trying to close him. The deal just faded away. We never did agree. I quit calling. His lawyers quit sending me revised drafts and I got on with my life. Lesson learned. Some deals aren't meant to be. I sold the idea to someone else.

It is important to realize that not every contact will pan out, and not every manager makes deals. Although the idea may seem a natural to you, and although the contact might enthusiastically agree with you, you still might not be able to come to an agreement. There can be internal political reasons; there can be personal reasons; or frankly, maybe they just don't have the dough and can't tell you. So don't waste your time chasing every opportunity. Sometimes you are wiser saving your shoe leather and telephone time by moving on.

To prevent a long, drawn-out drama from involving you, here's what you do. When you enter negotiations, set a time limit in your head. If nothing concrete happens by the end of this period, move on.

What should you expect to happen when you enter negotiations? If your idea is really any good, the company you're selling to should want to do something with it. More than one person will need to be called into a meeting at some time and the idea will be discussed seriously. As an idea gets tossed around, more and more people will get involved. If that isn't happening, your idea is not happening. It's going nowhere.

True, some deals do take a lot of work. If it's a highly involved contract, then give it some time to get ironed out. But don't let it drag on and on.

If you find yourself in that frustrating position – if you've given a fair amount of time for a deal's loose strings to get tied up but you're still in limbo – immediately go to the competition. Withdraw delicately from the first company and see if you can build a bonfire where the kindling is drier.

Remember what I said about risk? Some managers just can't tolerate any sort of risk. Even if they like your idea, you will find executives who just can't close. Sometimes it's fear: they won't be able to put their career on the line to support you. Sometimes it's political: office politics are deadly because you can't even begin to fathom what is happening inside their company. So you can do nothing about it.

You will begin to get a glimmer that things aren't going to end well when they start dragging their feet. Because they can't keep saying no forever, they will cook up a lot of excuses for the delay.

Perhaps they will put the blame on the stockholders: "Our stockholders expect us to pay a regular dividend and we can't afford the risk right now. Why don't you call back next month [or next year]?"

Maybe they will blame their budget: "It's a great idea, but we don't have any seed money to look into this right now. Why don't you come back in about three months, when the new budget is approved?"

Sometimes the reason for a delay isn't that they are timid, it's that they are smart. If they really like your idea, they can try to improve the terms by taking some of the sheen off the idea. They will start to find all kinds of things that are wrong with your idea. Then they can say, "How can you ask so much for something so flawed?" If it has no flaws, they have nothing to bargain with – and they will always try for a bargain. It's their job. So, even if they love it, they can't tell you that they love it. That way, you can't exploit their enthusiasm.

Running tests is a great way for them to make your idea look bad and to improve their negotiating position. The poorer the test result, the more they have to negotiate with.

To accomplish that, they will test your idea under the worst possible conditions. So you need to protect yourself. Here's how.

Most companies are constantly running tests of new concepts. These ideas are generated internally. When they say they will test your outside idea, they will slip it into some research that they already had scheduled. Because they are paying for the research, they get to ask the questions. They also get to determine the way they want the questions asked. They can select the people who do the testing. They can interpret the results and never even show them to you. They can stack the deck a million different ways.

If a company decides to play this game, I make them pay me for the privilege. The only time I allow a customer to test my idea is with an up-front fee *and* with me present at the test.

Why do I insist on this? Experience. Every time I have sold an idea being tested by a company, I was present. I took part. I got involved. Every time I was not allowed at the test, I didn't sell the idea. Isn't that strange?

I recall a focus group I attended with a research company I really liked. They were very understanding and cooperative. We had three groups of consumers look at the idea. I could see immediately I had big trouble with the first group interviewed. The moderator (the person asking the questions) didn't understand how the product worked, and he left it up to the consumers to figure it out. Some of them easily could, but others could not. They spent a lot of time discussing how the product should be used and spent most of the session discussing applications rather than judging its appeal. The results of that test were not very encouraging.

But that wasn't what we wanted to know. The test was supposed to find out whether the idea was a strong one, but the results from that first group only showed that the consumer didn't understand how to apply the product, not whether it was a good idea. The method of application wasn't important because the advertising campaign would show the consumer how to apply the product. Once the consumer saw the commercial, they would easily see how to apply it and there would be no confusion.

Somehow, this test had turned into something else. We were testing the wrong thing and getting results we didn't need. I had been talking with the marketing folks and the advertising agency, so I knew what the commercial was going to show. But I was the only one who knew that. That research company didn't. This meant I had to get involved.

After the first group had left, I spent some time with the moderator explaining what we were actually trying to find out. I explained how the product was to be applied. I showed him how to use it. I told him what the purpose of the test was. After he understood what the company actually wanted, it was as if we had an entirely different product. As you might imagine, the next two groups came back with entirely different results. Now everyone loved the idea. They really enjoyed using it. Everyone liked it, thought it was very useful, and said they would buy it.

If I had not been there, the research company would have reported the wrong results to my customer and they would have turned me down for the wrong reason – one that could easily have been handled in the advertising.

On another occasion, the results were fine but the interpretation of the results was flawed. Because I was there and had a copy of the report, I spotted the difficulty immediately and was able to put a positive spin on the outcome. As a result, instead of getting turned down flat and the matter being dropped, I was able to change a few things and correct the problem. The result was a sold product rather than a wasted one.

Remember, this is your baby and you should not let anyone take your baby away from you just so they can tinker around with it. They won't understand it the way you do, and the results they get will be flawed, or at least incomplete. You are the one who should guide this idea every step of the way. The minute you let go, your idea is sunk.

Negotiating is not solely about making a sale. Unless you sell all the rights outright (which will be discussed later), negotiating is also about keeping that income flowing. Your objective should be to sell something that will keep selling for years. To do that, you want to pick a company that will be around long enough to pay you. You want a strong customer, with prospects. Not only are strong companies going to be around longer but also they are easier to deal with. Companies in a decline don't want to change because they don't know what to do. They are confused by the changes they see around them and don't see a way out. As a result, they cling to the old tried-and-true methods of doing whatever it is they do.

I wouldn't recommend trying to sell anything to a company in decline or in a declining market. You will get a cool reception. Even if your idea is terrific, the executives won't budge. Consider this: If they can't recognize the trouble they are in, how can they recognize the value in your idea?

A company that is declining begins to dig in its heels and resists innovation. The people who are running it become more and more conservative as their business gets worse and worse. That means the managers of a company in decline certainly aren't going to be interested in a new idea. They can't even get rid of the old ones – that's why their business is declining. You must avoid companies like this at all costs. They are a dead end and they can ruin your invention.

What telltale signs should you look for? I can tell you this: Don't judge by the size of the offices or the number of people the company employs. Sheer size is very deceptive. Just because it is big doesn't make it a good company.

I once made a presentation to the largest manufacturer in its field. They were considered the eight-hundred–pound gorilla of the industry. They had plants all over the world. They had the most contracts. They had the biggest offices and the fattest bankroll. Frankly, I was salivating at the chance to get in to talk business with them.

I should have known better. When I got to the conference room, I found at least a dozen guys there. I was expecting a simple little presentation with the vice president of marketing, and instead I had half the new product development staff. At first, I was flattered. I wanted to think they were all eager to hear what I had to say. It was very gratifying. Unfortunately, they didn't want to hear a thing I had to say. They were using me, and I should have known it even before I entered the room.

I should have realized that something was seriously wrong when I passed through the marketing department on the way to the presentation. At the time, I didn't focus on it because I was already thinking about what I was going to say and I was eager to do a good job.

Now, this company was a giant. The marketing department itself was huge. The marketing department also was nice and quiet. It was so calm and dignified. The phone wasn't ringing. Things were very serene. No one was rushing around; no one was standing in the aisles. There was no buzz, no hum, no energy.

This should have registered immediately with me as a warning sign – these guys had nothing to do. They were the new-product development team, and they had nothing to do!

The quiet I heard was not because everything was running so smoothly. It was because the entire company was coasting. It was the eerie silence of lots of people just holding their breath and waiting.

Why were we holding a meeting about my idea? Because the VP of marketing was trying to motivate his staff by exposing them to something new: me. I was going to be fresh meat. But he was fighting an uphill battle. These guys were just sleepwalking and I was just an opportunity to make them look busy. This company was actually dead; its executives just didn't know it.

After I finished my presentation, the VP of marketing walked me to the door and thanked me again for coming. He assured me he would get back to me right away. I never heard from him again. Three months later, the company declared bankruptcy, fired its president for bribery, and laid off all the guys who were in that meeting. I would have liked to believe they'd been canned because of the way I was treated, but the reality was that the way I was treated was symptomatic of a company in big trouble.

My point is that you can't tell by the size of the offices how strong the business is. These guys at the dying behemoth were hanging on by a thread, and I should have seen it. I'd made a fundamental mistake: I hadn't thoroughly checked them out. I'd been so anxious to get in the door that I didn't sufficiently analyze whether it was even going to be a worthwhile trip. I'd gotten ahead of myself.

Here's a valuable clue by which to judge a company: Look at the company's product line and consider how actively it develops new products. A company with a management that is aware of changing markets is constantly innovating, constantly introducing new products. It is never positioned in a declining market. If you ask its managers about an older item that you haven't seen in a while, they will probably say, "We don't make that anymore. We discontinued it." That's why their business is growing. They trim out the deadwood instead of becoming a dead end.

From the moment you walk in the door, pay attention. If it's all very sedate and stately, be suspicious. Notice how many cubicles there are, and then notice how many are empty. Listen for the background hubbub of the telephone and the copy machine. Look for activity. It doesn't have to be a boiler factory; it can still be pleasant. But there must be something going on. I suppose the only really quiet place should be the CEO's office. He or she should be out of town, closing deals.

It's important to have the right client on the other end of the fishing line. It completely changes the type of presentation you make. You have to determine the attitude of the company as you walk in the door and from your initial contact. Some companies are run by calm, placid managers who like a steady ship. Some companies are full of pep and steam with lots of activity and energy. If a company is full of young lions ready to tear up the marketplace, I will toss my invention in the middle of them and duck. They will grab it in midair and start fighting over it. That's because they are competing with each other and you just might help them beat last year's numbers. You don't have to do a thing. The idea will practically sell itself. Unfortunately, this doesn't happen very often.

Most companies are not very hard driving. So if that's the case, don't just throw your idea out there and expect them to do anything. It will just lie on the floor. They are going to have to be wound up. You are the one who must do the winding. So your presentation has to be high energy and enthusiastic. Getting them to actively negotiate is going to take some doing.

I've found that one of the best methods for getting them to engage is to mention their competition somewhere in your presentation – right after the part about how much your product will increase market share. Unless they're asleep, you'll notice a head or two turn.

This brings me to the fundamental advantage that you enjoy, and one of which you may be unaware. The real reason they want to see what you have has nothing to do with you or your product. They just don't want their competition to see it first. What is actually driving them is not the benefit your product can bring but the damage your product can do if the competition has it. Your strongest sales point (which is generally unspoken) is running through their minds as you speak. Here you are selling your brains out, juggling pizza boxes and answering all their questions, and they are thinking, "Gee, what if the boys at R Boxes R Better get hold of this? It could really kill our box biz."

I know it's not very flattering to be asked in as a defensive measure, but there's a good chance that's why you got the meeting. Don't be insulted; it's still a great opportunity. It doesn't mean you can't make a sale. Once you are there, you can still be devastatingly effective. You've got a great idea here. Here's your chance to show it off with all its flags and banners flying. The important thing is to get your idea in front of the right people and give them the message. If you've done all your homework, as we've already discussed, they will listen. Getting them to pay attention is the single most important step toward getting them sold.

PART IV

Profiting from Your Idea

CHAPTER 14

The Rights You Should Sell

Once you have a patent, you can actually turn it into several different contracts. That's because a patent is made up of several claims, any or all of which can be sold to various people. So you can split your patent into little pieces and sell the rights to just one piece or another. And this can be very lucrative – if you do it right.

For instance, I have a number of patents in the gaming field. Companies are interested in buying the rights to these patents. Now, some of the claims in my patents are useful to state lotteries. Other claims deal with commercial applications such as fast-food restaurants that give away free items and cash as promotions. Commercial games are entirely different from state lotteries. One company interested in my patents is in the printing business for state lotteries – the company prints lottery tickets that are sponsored by a state. This company wouldn't be interested in the commercial rights to my patents, because that isn't the business the company is in. It just wants the lottery rights. So that's what I sell. I retain the commercial rights to sell to a different company that does commercial games and doesn't do state lotteries.

Your patent can be sold or licensed in different ways, too. You can sell exclusive rights or you can sell nonexclusive rights. Exclusive rights give the customer the unfettered right to use the patent and to keep anyone else from using it. Nonexclusive rights give the customer the unfettered right to use the patent but don't restrict you from selling those very same rights to someone else as well. This leaves you free to sell those same rights to someone else – perhaps even the first customer's competitor.

Why would any company settle for anything less than exclusivity?

It depends on the business. In the case of the lottery, a particular company has a long-term contract with certain states. Its competitors can't sell lottery ticket printing services to those states, so the customer doesn't need an exclusive on the patent. The customer already has a monopoly through its contract with its own customers, the specific states. Why should the customer pay for something it doesn't need? Exclusive rights are much more expensive and, in general, more valuable than nonexclusive rights. In this case, it's in the company's best interest to buy only nonexclusive lottery rights.

The company is happy because it gets just what it needs at a lower cost. You, the inventor, are happy because you get more than one customer providing you with royalties. And believe me, the numbers add up quickly. Jealously guarding your rights and selling only piecemeal can pay off handsomely, rewarding you for all the hard work you put into creating and marketing your idea.

So, how do you determine the right price and the right deal? There are about as many types of deals as there are inventors. Some want royalties. Some want up-front cash. And some want both. It's all over the board. Obviously, the right deal and the right price are going to vary from person to person and according to the customer's needs. It's a straightforward business decision, but you have to know what your options are.

Because there are so many nuances to this, I can't list all the possible deals, but I can give you an idea of some of the deals I've accepted and tell you why. While reading each of these cases, remember that you have both exclusive and non-exclusive rights to sell, and that exclusive rights are worth more because they give that customer the ability to keep other people from using those same rights. In other words, if they own the rights exclusively, they are the only company that can sell what you have.

Exclusive Rights

OUTRIGHT PURCHASE

You can sell the whole thing for cash or stock or something else that's valuable. This has lots of advantages. You don't have to worry about future litigation, defending your patent from infringement, or suing to prevent loss of claims. You don't have to worry about bookkeeping, working with people you don't like, holding a client's hand through the production and marketing phases, or (dare I say it?) failure of the idea to catch on.

There's only one disadvantage – you're out. If your idea becomes a blockbuster, you'll never see more from your deal than what you ink the first time. Or if your brilliant, beloved idea is mishandled by the buyer and never realizes its potential, there's nothing you can do about it. All you can do is let it go.

I've sold all rights to several patents outright, and sometimes, you know, it bothers me that I'm out of the game. I've seen companies just do absolutely nothing with the ideas I've sold them. I've seen other companies do quite well with my ideas. The frustrating thing is that you as the inventor can do nothing in either case. You are the guy who dreamed it up, and perhaps you can see a jillion different things that they should do, and they just don't see it. It's like standing at the dock and watching them run up the gangway and get on the wrong boat. You thought they were going on the *QE2* and they are rushing up the gangway to the *Titanic*.

Too bad; you are out of the game. Once you assign the rights to someone else, you are no longer the owner. It's like selling your car – it's no longer yours, it's theirs. You got paid. You're gone. But your heart is still attached, and it hurts to see your great idea toddle off into the sunset holding someone else's hand.

In all honesty, some companies only play ball this way. They want you gone. Ordinarily, it's not personal. It's just that they have a nice, comfortable little company and you're an outside irritant. The worst buyout I was ever in got really pretty nasty. The company executives couldn't wait to see me out of the deal. I was making way too many waves for them. They just wanted to get this idea safely locked away, unavailable to competitors, and go about their business. That idea never saw the light of day. Darn it!

How much should you ask for in an outright purchase deal? Well, the bad news is that if your idea really is a good one, an outright purchase will be the poorest deal. If it is a really big moneymaker and you've sold it all to a customer, you will never realize the full value from the patent. If you sell it for one hundred thousand dollars and it earns millions for the company, too bad for you. You can't very well go back and cry for more money – you would be laughed right out of the building.

And it's difficult to get a lot of money for an up-front deal. Think about it from the customer's point of view. A company's managers have stockholders and accountants to please. If they pay you a really large chunk of money, it will show up as a deduction in somebody's budget, so they will resist giving you a really large chunk of up-front money. It's a little easier if you'll take stock or something else that you might regard as valuable in lieu of cash.

On the other hand, inventors generally are completely unreasonable when it comes to money. Because it's their baby, as we've said many times, they think their idea is just the most valuable thing on earth. They want millions of dollars. It's silly. First of all, no one has millions to give you. It's just a single idea, for crying out loud. It's just a patent, not an entire business with hundreds of employees.

I suppose the idea of a patent being worth millions is based on the total earning power of the idea over the life of the patent. Remember, that's twenty years from the date of filing. A company has to be confident the patent will generate that kind of extra profit for all those years to afford to pay you big money.

As an example, let's say that the product generates ten million dollars in extra profit over the twenty years of the patent. Ten million dollars profit! That sounds like a lot of money, doesn't it? But over twenty years, that's only a half million dollars a year. They can't give it all to you now, can they? They bought your product to make money for their company. Shareholders are going to want to see this year's numbers beat last year's numbers.

So, how big a chunk of that five hundred thousand dollars can they give you and still help their bottom line? Obviously, they can't give you all of it. As a matter of fact, they can't even give you a small fraction of it. That's because no one knows if it will steadily make money every year for twenty years. It might do great for the first two years and then peter out. It's a lot like an oil well. It might start off like a gusher and a year later dry up. So, how much is too much?

Determining the sales price for a patent is also a function

of market risk. Company executives will consider how much it's going to cost them to take this idea to market. Production, sales, distribution... every department will have a piece of this. Depending on the product, it can be very expensive to introduce it to the market. There are lots of extra, one-time expenses, such as sales meetings, introductory commercials, and new media buys. There are samples and coupons and special dealer allowances to get on the shelf, and...

Well, you get the idea. These all have to be funded, in addition to the inventor's buyout package. And, sadly, even though you have convinced them that this idea is just terrific, they still are taking a substantial risk that it will flop. You will be long gone and they will have egg all over their faces. As you might imagine, this has a negative effect on the buyout price. So what's an eager inventor going to do?

In general, you should weigh the expected yearly increase that your idea will bring to the customer's business, and then multiply that by some number representing the period of years during which the idea will sustain the increase. This is very similar to the way Wall Street analysts value companies. Companies are valued by taking their per-share earnings (their earnings divided by the number of shares) times some multiple. The multiple varies from business to business. It can be ten or less for solid, not very fast-moving and conservative companies, such as banks or insurance firms. It can be forty or more for zippy software companies with terrific growth potential and skyrocketing profits. Look at your idea in the same way.

So, which is your idea – a stodgy, solid idea or a zippy skyrocket? If your idea will have a profound effect on the company's business, you could be talking about a substantial sales price. But if your idea's just a good, solid improvement, then it's going to be tough to ask for that.

Now, here is another one of those absolutely important points you must ingrain in your brain: The tougher you are, the tougher it gets.

Imagine that. All this work and effort and you drop the ball at the very last moment by being (need I say it?) greedy.

The people you're selling your idea to can get around your patent, you know. They aren't stupid. A good engineer and a good lawyer can slide around your patent like oil. The only reason they are talking to you is because it's easier to buy it from you in a completed form than to have to figure a way around you, which could be tricky. If they did work around you, then they'd take the risk that you might sue (or have their competition sue), and you'd both wind up in court instead of in the marketplace, where you want to be. So, you see, their interest in dealing with you at all boils down to one issue: the amount of effort you can save them. You're expedient, not indispensable.

In general, I'm conservative and just negotiate for a substantial check. That may be because I have done this before and know I can do it again. I can return to my well of creativity and come up with a new salable patent. I'm not tied to just one buggy. This mindset helps me sit back and evaluate things differently. And it has its benefits. The way you fashion any deal can affect your future negotiations. If the customer thinks you're easy to deal with, then it might make it easier for you to come back with your next idea. Also, when dealing with other clients, there is no better endorsement of your ability than a sold patent. Think of it as advertising. It says your ideas are good enough for someone to pay you for them.

A final thought on this matter: Haggling is a two-way street. The tougher you are in any negotiation, the harder the customer is going to try to squeeze you. In many cases, this can be self-defeating. By being stubborn, you can end up just making it tougher on yourself.

The outright purchase is common because most companies don't want a long-term relationship with you; they just want you out of there. They own the rights; you don't own anything. Any other deal starts to get complicated. They don't like complicated deals because they make for misunderstandings and bad feelings.

LICENSE

The next simplest deal, after the outright purchase, is a license. A license just says the customer can use your idea and will pay you some agreed-upon fee on an annual basis. There is no other compensation. There might be an escape clause after a certain term, which allows either you or the company to end the deal at any time with thirty- or sixty-day or some other agreed-upon notice. This is actually a fair way to do it. If the product bombs, the company doesn't want to pay you for something that's useless. If the product is great, the company doesn't want you to shut it down without plenty of warning.

I usually settle for a five-year minimum and an option to renew the license every three years or so. It can vary depending on the client. This gives you a guaranteed minimum: your annual license fee multiplied by the minimum license period. I must warn you, though, that this will likely cap your potential income from the idea, because under a licensing deal the specified compensation generally is all you'll get.

The nature of the business world itself can get involved in your negotiations, too, and you'd be wise to pay attention to it. Companies are incredibly volatile. The people you did business with in signing your contract aren't going to be around at the end of the license period. The norm is for brand managers to change every year and CEOs to change every five years. Everybody else in the chain of command will likely turn over between those two extremes, and after about five years – when your license comes up for renewal – you probably will have a whole new team to deal with and to resell on your idea.

Reselling is not difficult if your idea is continuing to make lots of money for the company. But if it's just OK or (perish the thought) not doing so well, then the new team will probably cancel. Then you must reshop the concept. Unfortunately, now the idea has been used, so it will be a lot more difficult to sell to the competition. If your idea hasn't done well, you will have real trouble getting any more out of it unless you can show that the original company didn't handle it very well. Even if your idea does really well, chances are that in a few years competitors will have something in the field that is similar, and that will start hurting your sales.

No one knows what the future holds. People and circumstance change, so hanging your future income on the future puts you at more risk.

UP-FRONT PAYMENT AND ROYALTIES

The next simplest deal is an up-front payment and royalties. You've heard of this, I'm sure. It sounds like every inventor's dream, because it compensates you immediately and also promises ongoing income. But what you may not realize is that the up-front payment is generally fairly modest, and the royalty payment is always tiny.

Why such parsimony from the buyer? Well, the up-front will be modest because you are shifting the risk to the company. You have its money, no matter what happens to the product. You must be prepared to accept less compensation in connection with your lowered risk. Meanwhile, your royalty is going to be built into the price of the product. If the price becomes too high, it will make the product less attractive to consumers, and in the long run, you will lose sales and royalties.

How much you should ask for in an up-front payment and royalty rate depends, again, on the impact of the product. You have to deduct zeros from the up-front because you are (hopefully) getting royalties, too, and (hopefully) these payments will go on and on for twenty years. You should certainly recoup all your costs for developing, protecting, and selling your idea – which can add up to quite a bit – and include a very nice piece of change for yourself.

The royalty amount can vary, so you can take more up front for a lower royalty or less up front for a more generous royalty. Royalties are rarely more than 5 percent of sales and generally are 1 percent or 2 percent. It really depends upon the market you are in, the price of the product, and the condition of the company. A really big market and a high price for the product will sustain a larger royalty.

But know this: Royalties can be a pain.

Although you might be dreaming of a contract for an up-front and royalties, the truth is that companies generally hate this kind of deal because it is a pain to administer, and companies like to keep things clean. If a company signs an agreement to pay royalties, you will have to conduct semiannual (or even monthly) audits of the sales to determine royalty payments. You have to hire an auditor. The company has to open its books. It gets to be a hassle. And it goes on and on, year after year.

I only got this kind of deal once, and I ended up in a law-suit. So, even though an up-front-plus-royalties arrangement sounds like heaven, I hate it, too. Imagine that! The thing every would-be inventor dreams about is probably their biggest nightmare.

Nonexclusive Rights

All of the numbers above should be adjusted downward for deals selling nonexclusive rights. It's obvious why. This kind of agreement lets you sell your idea again and again to other customers. But there is tremendous earning potential for you if you go this route and manage your business in a shrewd fashion.

If you sell nonexclusive rights, you should do everything in your power to cut as many deals as you can and to make the payments as small as you can in good conscience accept. After all, you're going to make it up on the volume, so to speak. It is far better to have your patent diversified. Remember the renewal conundrum – if you sign to renew your contract every five years (which is pretty standard), then every five years you will have to face the music once again. Better to have the money continue to flow in from a fair number of deals than to be locked into only a few deals that could burn out after five years.

And there's another advantage to selling your idea to a number of companies. If you have several using your idea, none of them can back away from it, because none can let the competition beat it out. It puts pressure on each company to keep paying you. This gets even more acceptable to the company if its payment to you is small enough to be consid-ered only a minor budgetary nuisance.

I have used each of the deals listed above. Again, they

vary per idea, per customer, and per field. Some deals might not apply to the field for your idea. Some might not be usable down the road because times are always changing. But the style is what is important here. The flavor of the deal is what you should notice.

CHAPTER 15

The Deals Devils Do

We all wish that your client, having seen the brilliant light of your wonderful idea, would meekly sign a generous agreement with you and give you everything that is fair and honest and easy to work with.

That's a nice dream. I have never experienced it, however. Perhaps it's harder to realize than I would hope.

I will now tell you something you probably always suspected, even if you've so far been spared the evidence of it: Lawyers can be very tricky. That's what their clients pay them for.

By "tricky" I don't necessarily mean dishonest. I mean that lawyers are very experienced in getting the most for their clients. They do it every day. You don't. If you think you are going to be able to negotiate an agreement without having legal counsel look over your final agreement, you should think again.

Every contract has its quirks, and the inexperienced can be blind to them. Let's consider licensing agreements. The tricky part is how these items get worded. I have been around the barn a few times with these deals, so I can give you my perspective, which it is hoped will keep you from staying up nights kicking yourself.

Obviously, you want royalties, but how do these royalties get calculated? Let's say the royalty is 2 percent – but 2 percent of what? It is important that your deal be fair, but it is also important that your deal be verifiable – the final amount must be based on a real number that can be calculated by your accountant. To show you what I mean, let's look at one of my recent contracts.

I wanted to get paid on every item that was manufactured. The amount was based on count, not profit. I wanted so much per item and I didn't care what the end user was charged for it. Why? Because actual production of an item can be tracked. If it has weight and size, it can be measured and a rough measure can be determined from shipping bills of lading. If an item's being manufactured, then production records can be examined to get a fair estimate of volume. All this is verifiable.

But, you may ask, isn't profit verifiable? Nope. The fact is that most businesses charge large customers one price, smaller customers another, close customers a third, and old customers yet another. And then there are promotional offers and special deals and stocking allowances and... Well, darn it, it's tough to figure out who is making how much on what. There is a somewhat pejorative term for all these profit shenanigans: Hollywood accounting.

The term arises from the old movie studios' way of calculating payments to script authors and actors who owned a percentage of the profit. Moviemakers' accounting practices became so flagrant they defied logic. The accountants at the studios would deduct all kinds of things before calculating the profit. There was depreciation on the lot, sound stage, and equipment, and then rehearsal time had to be factored in. Sound studios, catering, cars, trailers... On and on until no matter how much money the movie made, there were no profits! It could be a megablockbuster... and no profits. It could have lines of eager theatergoers wrapping around the block... no profits. It could win eleven Academy Awards, have critics raving, millions of adoring fans who would willingly see it again and again. No matter... no profits. Hollywood accounting.

See what I mean? Now, your customers wouldn't do that to you, would they? Well, just to be on the safe side, I'd be careful. Base your payment on something that is easily verifiable, even if it means you won't make quite as much. Chalk it up to giving a little to get a lot better night's sleep and to avoid very expensive and ugly lawsuits.

You probably already know that nearly every snag you will hit during the negotiating process is ultimately going to come down to money. For that reason, I know that a lot of inventors just refuse to deal with it. They want to stick their heads in the sand and hope it will go away.

Don't. With a little planning, you can protect yourself and your sanity. There are some general rules to obey. We'll start with a story about a partnership.

A while ago, I had a really large project with a partner. Partnerships are usually difficult arrangements, but this one was the exception. I absolutely loved this guy. He was honest. He was fair. He did more than I expected. I thought I was very lucky. My share was always sent to my bank on time and in exactly the right amount. No problem.

Then, at the end of the program, there was one last payment. It didn't come. I waited. It never showed up. I called my partner, and the essence of the discussion went like this:

Me: "Hey, where's the last payment?"

He: "What payment?"

Me: "The last payment."

He: "There is no last payment."

Me: "*What?*"

My partner then went back over all the numbers, and when we got to the issue of the last payment, he tried to make the case that I had somehow said that he could keep the last payment to cover some improvements to his office, which he'd had to make to handle the job.

I didn't recall saying any such thing. I did recall saying that he could hold the money for a while until the checks started coming in, because otherwise he'd have to put out money up front. To me, that was not the same as giving him a very substantial gift of the last payment, which ran into some pretty big money.

Well, it got pretty ugly. We had a meeting and I ended up shouting and pounding on the table. He was yelling about taking a lie-detector test. Gee, it was… unpleasant. (And this was the partner from heaven I had been so glad to have!)

We finally settled the matter, but it really screwed up a good team. I regret it to this day.

There are several rules of thumb you should use when preparing that final contract:

- You should try to keep your deals normal and avoid unusual deals.
- You should try to limit your liability to things that you actually can control.
- You should always specify dates and spell out when something is supposed to happen.
- You should try to keep at arm's length from your client.
- You should insist on an up-front payment.
- You should look out for hidden penalties.
- You should negotiate with as few people as possible.

Avoid Unusual Deals

Unusual deals, exceptions to the usual flow of business, are to be avoided. For instance, if someone needs some cash to complete his side of a deal, don't lend it to him. It will just come back to haunt you.

A lawyer will not understand an unusual deal, and that very fact will annul the reason you are paying a lawyer in the first place: for the expertise. Lawyers have experience with normal deals. An unusual one is outside their area of expertise. Why risk it? Furthermore, clients will not understand your interpretation of an unusual deal, either. Business is dynamic. What was very important at one time is inconsequential the next. The reason you might make an unusual deal will probably not even apply at the end, so everyone will wonder why it was done that way.

Now, this might make you feel like you are being very hard-nosed to demand standard, straightforward deals. You are not. In the long run, you are protecting all parties. Unusual deals outside the usual format of business always end up in misunderstandings. That's why they're unusual.

Limit Your Liability

When it comes to finally scrawling your signature on a contract, you should have endeavored to limit your liability. Because you own the rights or the patent, you have to defend that patent or lose the rights. But you are just a single individual and your customer is a big company; why is it up to you? Because that's what you are selling—you are selling rights to the monopoly. If someone violates your patent, you must defend it. At least, that's what your customer will say.

But when the negotiations reach this subject, know this: You don't have to defend your patent with your last drop of blood.

A patent defense can cost an awful lot of money, but you don't have to expose yourself to potential bankruptcy. You can limit the amount you would have to pay for such a legal defense by putting it into the contract. Limit your liability to the amount you have received in royalties. That way, even if you get into a really difficult situation during litigation, you can never lose more than your customer has paid you. You might end up not making any money on your idea, but you won't lose more money than you've already been paid for it.

Specify Dates

Specifying dates is another critical rule to follow when settling on your compensation. If you base all your payment on verifiable units, be sure to specify *when and how often* you get paid. Why?

Let's suppose that things start off slow. What do you do in a case where there are no verifiable units? What if there are no sales? What if the company just sits on your patent and doesn't do anything with it? You have a deal – you can't sell it again – but your wonderful idea is in a state of suspended animation, as good as dead. If you haven't put in a specific date and a specific amount that is due no matter what, you could find yourself waiting in vain for the postman to come, and get no check... ever.

Now, your client wouldn't do that to you, would it? Sure. Why not? It has gotten you out of the way at no cost. In light of this trap, you must insist that you receive payment according to some schedule of dates. You must also make sure that if the customer defaults on those payments, it loses the rights to the patent.

Remember, the only things you have to sell are your rights. Use them like a weapon to make sure the customer will do what you want. Just because the customer wants the rights doesn't grant it the ability to control you.

You can insist that your customer produce the goods, of course, but in the long run, that may not be in your best interest. After all, maybe the market is not ready for your idea, or perhaps the product can't be put together in time. There can be a lot of legitimate factors that keep a product off the market. But as long as you get paid, why should you care? Just make sure that there is a minimum payment due to you every few months (or every month) after a certain point, so you can keep the pressure on the company to manufacture and sell. If they elect not to, that's fine. You still get paid.

Keep at Arm's Length

Let's say your customer does a poor job of producing your idea and somebody sues it for sloppy manufacturing. It could happen, you know. Your wonderful idea could end up being the basis for a lawsuit. Any lawyer worth his or her salt will name everyone possible in a lawsuit – the manufacturer, the retailer, and of course, you. So here we are again, defending a lawsuit. You didn't do anything wrong. All you did was dream up an idea and sell it to someone who didn't do a good job. Your arrangement with your customer didn't stipulate that the way the customer made your idea into a product would be safe or useful.

Fortunately, you can avoid this problem by an "arm's-length agreement" that basically says you cannot be held responsible for any use made of the product, nor for any damage caused by its manufacturing or distribution. Your involvement should be limited to the patent rights, and that's it. This limit keeps you above any battle that might begin. All you did was sell the rights; what happens after that is not your affair.

This same philosophy applies to your personal time after selling the rights to your idea. In most cases, the customer will want to use you to explain the idea to their people. There will be meetings – lots of meetings. You will have to fly to their plant in Brazil. There will be shots for swamp fever – very expensive shots. If you don't specify an arm's-length agreement, lots of other demands on your time can appear, because you aren't free of this patent. So, before you set yourself up for that sort of grief, you must make sure the agreement keeps you out of the extra duties following the sale. From your point of view, all you are selling is the patent, not your indentured servitude.

Now, you *can* work out some sort of employment agreement. As a matter of fact, I encourage it. Your expertise can be very helpful in getting your idea off the ground properly, in trim and fully fueled with just the right stuff to get it into orbit. Your input can be very important. Just keep it separate from the sales contract. The employment agreement will say that you will get paid for your time, travel, and expenses. You can specify that you expect to fly first class. You can demand that you stay only in the best hotels. You can even request a limo at your beck and call (but you probably won't get it).

The employment agreement is usually a normal enough arrangement by which the customer pays you by the job or by the hour at a stated rate. It will cover travel and expenses. (Be aware, though, that the customer will probably use the company travel agent and book you on planes and in hotels just as if you were a regular employee.)

If you want to see your idea implemented – thus bearing fruit for your customer and increasing your own status as an inventor – then it's probably a good idea to work for your customer in promoting it. But, again, the employment agreement must be separate from the patent agreement.

INSIST ON AN UP-FRONT PAYMENT

As the saying goes, "Time is money." Your time is valuable. To doubly ensure you are compensated for the time you've sunk into your idea, you are fully entitled to a payment at the very beginning of your contractual relationship.

Yes, the bulk of your money from your idea may come in royalties, but the customer still should pay you at signing. This is to cover your time in developing and presenting the idea in the first place. The up-front should be something substantial enough that if your idea flops, or if it can't be made or never sells, you won't feel you wasted your time. An up-front is customary. Don't let anyone tell you otherwise.

Even if your contract doesn't pay royalties, you should still demand an up-front that is separate from the first payment of an outright purchase. The up-front should always be independent of the rollout of the product or of any sales. You should get paid simply for signing.

Look Out for Hidden Penalties

The business of signing on the bottom line can be full of twists to the very end, so look out for hidden penalties.

I once had a deal in which the lawyer who drafted the contract went out of his way to slip in a penalty clause. It wasn't in the first two drafts of the agreement, but there it was in the third, plain as day. The clause said that if for some reason I did not defend my patent and the customer was forced to defend it, and further, if my customer defended it and lost, I had to pay triple the customer's outlay for legal defenses as a penalty.

Now, ordinarily, a licensing agreement between parties, like any other contract, implies that both parties trust each other to do the right thing. There was no reason for my customer to slip in such a clause.

I went nuts! I didn't sign, of course. As a matter of fact, I never dealt with that company again. Why would anyone try something like that?

Well, first, it wasn't the lawyer's idea. No lawyer would do that unless his or her client had requested it. Remember, the client is calling the shots, not the lawyer. I therefore realized that the company execs themselves didn't want me to sign. They wanted to be able to say that they were willing to sign me up but that I was being difficult.

It turns out that I had gotten crosswise of a bitter political battle between the president and the senior vice president. The senior VP was championing my patent, but the president controlled the lawyer. No way was the senior VP going to get what he wanted without coming through the president. I was just caught in the middle. The deal was a victim of politics. Sort of a tragedy.

Well, actually, it wasn't a tragedy. Two years later, the company went under. Had I signed, my idea would have been buried in the wreckage.

The foregoing is a good example of how matters completely unrelated to your idea can rope you into unfair agreement terms. You must be wary of these personal motives and hidden political agendas that have nothing to do with you but that can still put you in a terrible position. Such machinations, unfortunately, are a large component of the business world. Businesses, after all, are run by human beings with emotions that, in retrospect, make you wonder how rational we all are.

Negotiate With as Few People as Possible

The human factor represents another potential pitfall. Therefore, in working on your contract, try to keep the number of different people in the approval chain as limited as possible. The more people who have to handle the document, the murkier and more difficult it will get. Everyone has a pet peeve or special spin he or she wants to see in it. If any of these people then moves on, as frequently occurs in today's business world, the folks left behind will hardly know why the special spin or pet peeve was put in the contract in the first place. There will be language in the contract that no one can remember wanting, and they won't know why it is there.

What you want is a nice, simple deal that everyone can understand and that everyone feels comfortable with. The best way to get anything approved is to make sure it doesn't have to rest on many desks. Keep it simple, and keep it small. Keeping in mind that fewer is better will help make your deal short and sweet.

CHAPTER 16

From Contact to Contract

As you look back over the territory we've covered, you might wonder whether all of this is actually going to be worth doing. It is a lot of work to take your initial idea from a little glimmer of a thought all the way to a money-gushing dynamo. In most cases, the work is well worth the effort because it validates your faith in yourself and in your idea. It's gratifying to see your product on the shelf. It's nice to be able to take credit for a great idea. The money is certainly nice, too.

Taking your invention from inception to sale is a real journey – as real as paddling up the Amazon and back. You will learn a lot about yourself and others along the way. You will return from the trip a changed person. Some things will be much easier than you now imagine them to be, some will present more problems than you expected, but all will have been interesting.

The important thing to bear in mind is that you can stop at any time. No one is going to be holding a gun to your head. You don't have to do any of it. The more you do, the less expensive it will be for you, but there is a host of people who will be glad to take over – all you have to do is pay them.

If you do decide to farm out some of the work, be prepared to get an inferior job. As we've discussed, nothing can substitute for an inventor's enthusiasm. Companies don't like dealing with intermediaries because they actually are relying as much on the inventor's insight and ability as on the product itself. Being represented by someone else places a barrier between the client and the inventor. Some of the spontaneity is missing. It also takes away a lot of the fun.

Fun? Yes, it actually is fun. Bear in mind that it's just an idea, not brain surgery. The world got along just fine without your idea before you came up with it, and it can get along just fine without your idea after you've come up with it. Making your idea into a product or selling the process is something that you might want to do, but as we've said, at first it will just be you. If the process is distasteful, you don't have to go forward. You can pull the string and stop it at any time.

Inventing products is a sole proprietorship. You're the boss. You call all the shots. You decide what to do and what not to do. For some people, that is a lot of fun, but not everyone will see it that way. This book should give you an idea about what you are really going to find out there. These are things that I've run into. I didn't anticipate a lot of the attitudes that I discovered, and I assume that if they were new to me, they will be new to you.

There probably are a lot of things you will run into that I've somehow managed to avoid. The nice part about this business is that we aren't competitors; we're actually partners. The chance of you coming up with something that is going to be competitive with my ideas is remote. So we can help each other. At least, that's what I hope you'll have found in this book.

It's quite a trip, taking an idea from its initial form to a contract form. Your idea will change along the way, and so will you.

ABOUT THE AUTHOR

Stuart J. Kamille began his business career in the advertising and marketing industry in 1969. He subsequently held posts ranging from copywriter to creative director to director of sales promotion and executive vice president, working on high-profile Fortune 500 and multinational corporation accounts. As senior vice president of Los Angeles-based Simon Marketing in 1977, Kamille developed and produced the first fast-food game for McDonald's Corporation. Games based on his idea are still run throughout the world.

In 1984, Kamille formed Winner's Selection, Inc., a sales promotion company. In 1987, he successfully developed and patented the largest sales promotion program in history – the Millionaire Cash Quiz – for RJR/Nabisco. The promotion included 3.2 billion game pieces, which required sixty railway cars of paper and took six months to print.

Kamille is a frequent guest lecturer at the University of Georgia's Terry College of Business in Athens, Georgia, and the Reynolds School of Journalism at the University of Nevada, Reno.

Kamille holds eight U.S. and international patents in such diverse fields as mathematics, lottery gaming, and electronic scoring and analysis. He frequently advises clients on employee creativity and motivation. He is the author of several books dealing with innovation and creativity and sales. His books are available from www.atlasbooks.com and www.stuartjkamille.com.

CPSIA information can be obtained at www.ICGtesting.com
Printed in the USA
BVOW11s0225280915

419932BV00011B/93/P

9 780977 473502